New Wineskins

STUDIEN ZUR INTERKULTURELLEN GESCHICHTE DES CHRISTENTUMS
ETUDES D' HISTOIRE INTERCULTURELLE DU CHRISTIANISME
STUDIES IN THE INTERCULTURAL HISTORY OF CHRISTIANITY

Herausgegeben von/edité par/edited by

Richard Friedli   Walter J. Hollenweger   Hans Jochen Margull
Université de Fribourg   University of Birmingham   Universität Hamburg

Band 30

Verlag Peter Lang
FRANKFURT AM MAIN · BERN

Joyce V. Thurman

NEW WINESKINS
A Study of the
House Church Movement

Verlag Peter Lang
FRANKFURT AM MAIN · BERN

CIP-Kurztitelaufnahme der Deutschen Bibliothek

Thurman, Joyce V.:

New wineskins : a study of the House Church
Movement / Joyce V. Thurman. - Frankfurt am
Main ; Bern : Lang, 1982.
  (Studien zur interkulturellen Geschichte
  des Christentums ; Bd. 30)
  ISBN 3-8204-7172-3
NE: GT

ISSN 0170-9240
ISBN 3-8204-7172-3
© Verlag Peter Lang GmbH, Frankfurt am Main 1982

Druck und Bindung: fotokop wilhelm weihert KG, darmstadt

CONTENTS

Dedication   6

Acknowledgements   7

Preface   8

Chapter 1:   Some Trends of the Past Twenty Years   11

Chapter 2:   The History of the Movement   23

             The Harvestime Churches   24
             The North Churches   30
             The Church at South Chard   34

Chapter 3:   Selective Case Histories   37

             The Harvestime Group
             1. Chester - The Church of the Way   37
             2. The Solihull Christian Fellowship   40
             3. The Church at Merryfield House, Witney   43

             The North Fellowships
             1. The Russell House Fellowship, Leamington Spa   47
             2. The Wake Green Road Fellowship, Moseley, Birmingham   52

             The Influence of the Church at South Chard   56

Chapter 4:   Life in the House Church   61

Chapter 5:   Historical Comparisons of the House Church Movement
             with Early Methodism, Brethrenism and the Early
             Pentecostals   75

             Methodism   75
             The Brethren   81
             The Pentecostals   85

Chapter 6:   The Place and Future of the House Church   93

Notes   103

Bibliography   107

TO DAVID AND ANDREW

ACKNOWLEDGEMENTS

I wish to thank Prof. W.J. Hollenweger for his constant encouragement and help, and also to express my appreciation to him and to Mrs W.J. Hollenweger for the hospitality of their evening seminars.

I am grateful to all those in the House Churches who gave so unselfishly of their time in order to give me information and answer my questions.

I am greatly indebted to Mrs I. Browne for her efficient typing of the text and her help in the practical matters of publication.

My thanks go also to Dr Hugh McLeod of the University of Birmingham, who was my supervisor during the research and preparation of this work. He first encouraged me onto the exciting paths of research.

To Mrs J. Pearce, Secretary to Prof. W.J. Hollenweger, my deep thanks for all the kindness and practical advice she has given me over the years.

Finally, to my husband David and son Andrew my thanks and gratitude for all their enthusiasm, encouragement and patience.

The House Church Movement in Britain numbers several hundred churches
with over 50,000 members. They have come into existence within a short period
of about ten years at a time when most denominations have had to face a de-
crease in membership and many have had to give up some of their church
buildings.

The house churches grew out of the conviction that the existing church
system, be it Anglican or Free Church, is unlikely to be renewed. The old
wineskins cannot hold the new wine of the revival. The traditional liturgies
are a hindrance for a proper teaching ministry and the evangelical sermon
does not fulfil its function as a missionary tool. Therefore, other tools
have to be shaped.

These other tools were partly provided by the Charismatic Movement.
"The leaders of the House Church Movement were never themselves associated
with any group promoting charismatic renewal (such as the Fountain Trust)
but arrived at their position on the nature of the church independently.
Nevertheless the ranks have been swelled by disillusioned members of churches
who have become impatient waiting for the denominational structures to experience revival" (p. 86).

Like the Methodists, the Salvation Army and the Pentecostals, who all
tried to revive the existing churches, the House Church Movement is the
result of a failed attempt at reviving the existing churches and thus will
become - not immediately, but in time - another denomination.

As the name indicates, the meetings of the House Church Movement began
in private houses. Now, however, the movement has expanded into larger
premises such as school halls and churches which have been bought from the
traditional denominations. Three main types of house churches have originated
independently of each other and of the mainstream of the Charismatic Movement.

These chains of house churches have no central organisation and do not
want to be known by any of the names under which Joyce Thurman lists them.
Normally they are simply known by the name of their local church. Nevertheless, each of the three chains has a distinctive character and has strong
and identifiable links which are secured not through the normal forms of
ecclesiastical administration but through the itinerant ministry of their
leaders, through common conferences and a common stock of hymns and choruses,
through a chain of highly successful shops, common behaviour patterns, and
visits between the churches. These create a strong link of a mycelial nature. This hardly visible subterranean network explains why suddenly and
apparently spontaneously house churches are mushrooming in different parts
of the country and following the same pattern. In short, the House Church
Movement displays all the features of oral culture which are known through
the study of pre-literary cultures in the Third World and through formge-
schichte in Biblical research. We find here behaviour and communication

patterns, and ways of communication which seem to be very similar across the
centuries and the oceans.

That is all the more interesting as the majority of the members of the
house churches are not "illiterates" or "semi-literates". In fact they are
thoroughly middle-class, married couples with young children, families at
the peak of their life. In every local church there is a high proportion
of university graduates, medical doctors, industrial executives, solicitors,
teachers, nurses and social workers. Whether a group behaves according to
an "oral" or "literary" behaviour pattern has very little to do with their
educational level.

Much care is taken in the teaching of new members and in the teaching
of the children. The house church members know what they believe and why.
There is an absence of the traditional gospel-type sermon - "a fundamental
difference from the denominational evangelical churches" (p. 68). The sermon
(lasting between one and two hours) has a teaching function for church members. Mission and evangelism is not carried out through public speeches and
sermons but rather on a personal one to one contact.

Theologically the three chains in the House Church Movement which Joyce
Thurman discusses represent three traditions of the Pentecostal movement,
without having any connexion with any of the existing Pentecostal organisations. The Harvestime Churches stand in the mainstream of Pentecostal
tradition. That they have not joined any of the Pentecostal denominations
is an indication that conformity of theology does not create unity (or even
ecumenical relationships). What an important insight for our ecumenical
committees! The chain depending from South Chard tends towards a sort of
"Jesus only" Pentecostalism, whilst Mr North's interpretation of the New
Birth is well known within a certain perfectionist type of Pentecostalism.

Joyce Thurman ends her investigation with the following uncomfortable
statement:

> "The institutional structures of the denominations were built
> to serve the mass of society, not cater for an exclusive
> grouping.... [However] the future of Christianity will lie
> with those deeply committed to a sectarian faith who will
> survive through de-Christianisation processes." (p. 104)

I consider this to be an over-statement. To date no society could survive
without an organisation which served the masses and gave society a kind of
general religious framework. The question, however, is whether a church
which tries to fulfil this general, stabilising function in society, can at
the same time cater for the small groupings who are searching for more in
Christianity than a general orientation. If this is not the case then we
necessarily need different types of churches, those formed on the principle
of a person to person fellowship and those formed on the needs of society
at large. The ecumenical problem will then not be so much how the different
(Catholic, Anglican, Reformed, Methodist) denominations relate to each other
(from our point of view they all fulfil sociologically the same function) but
how they relate to "the denominations of the future", that which sociologists

call the "sect-type" of Christianity, of which the House Churches are an important expression.

That indeed is a task for which our normal ecumenical structures are singularly unprepared as most of them still work within traditional theological and denominational divides. These divides are almost irrelevant when it comes to the problem of the ecumenical relationship between house churches and the more traditional denominations (including the organisationally more advanced Pentecostal denominations).

In understanding this relationship (or better: lack of relationship) so-called non-theological factors are much more important, as for example the answer to the question: Who can be a leader, a priest, a pastor in the church? The House Churches answer this question by justifying their existing, formally untrained, but highly professional "lay leaders". The denominations answer this question by justifying their existing, formally trained and ordained, but in many cases unprofessional clergy. Thus the root of their argument is not their theological conviction but the necessity to defend an organisation with which they are landed whether they like it or not.

One can therefore question the terminology of "non-theological" factors as these factors are theologically very relevant. Normally, however, one identifies the causes which divide House Churches from denominations in the fields of culture, social behaviour, and access to leadership.

The work of Joyce Thurman (which was carried out under the supervision of my colleague Dr Hugh McLeod) demands an ecumenical theology which does not relegate the "cultural" and the "social" to the realm of the "non-theological" and therefore to the theologically irrelevant. It demands a theology which, using the tools of intercultural theology, discovers the theological and ecumenical significance of these so-called "non-theological" factors.

Joyce Thurman has not tackled this task. But by presenting a picture of that part of church history which goes on under our noses (without us recognising it) she invites us to see the divide between "oral" and "literary" Christianity even in the midst of Britain and to see this divide as a challenge for intercultural theology within our own culture.

Dr Walter J. Hollenweger,
Professor of Mission,
University of Birmingham.

The rapid scientific and technological changes of this century have led to a development of human power never previously envisaged. From the advances in space exploration to the fact that most of the material goods used today have been developed in the past eighty years, such things point to the fact that man is indeed master of his environment. This is a world in which the sacred appears to have no authority, the secular alone is relevant and religion is no longer an important sociological factor.

Traditional beliefs are superseded as society acknowledges a general secularisation. This has resulted in a religious crisis to which there can be seen two principal reactions:

1. To embrace the changing society and consider secularisation as a necessary and welcome development. This is the standpoint of modern theology.

2. To react hostilely to such a process, viewing it as an attack upon the sovereignty of God.

The evangelical sections of the church (in which tradition stands the House Church Movement) believe that the response to secularisation lies in a return to a pattern of life based on biblical standards, coupled with the establishment of authority in church and family life.

Each post-war theologian has attempted to interpret the Christian faith and tenets to the modern man. Tillich saw God as "the ground of our being"; Bultmann reinterpreted Christian statements by processes of demythologisation and Bonhoeffer spoke of a religionless Christianity.

In this country the radical ideas exploded in the form of a book written in a popular vein by the then Bishop of Woolwich, John Robinson. Perhaps the book's most significant contribution was that it brought those ideas to the attention of the thinking public, and provided an alternative to the anthropomorphic ideas of Christianity which had existed for so long.

One can argue effectively that religion has not in fact declined, that there never existed a truly religious age. The events of history show religion and politics were always so intertwined that the truly devout were always in a minority. The members of the House Churches can be equated in their wholehearted zeal with deviants such as the Lollards in the medieval scene.

The radical theologian sees the demythologisation of Christian ideas as a satisfactory means of reconciling or accommodating Christian faith to the support of a scientific world view. In contrast those in the House Churches will constantly emphasise the continuing supernatural intervention of God both in the world, allowing and controlling events, and in the daily life of the believer.

An identification with the modern world is understood by the theologian, whereas the House Church Movement holds a strong sectarian approach. The church is a bulwark against the world, its members are separate and secure against the threats of the secular society.

There is a tendency for radical theologians to be influenced by social movements. A deep concern is felt by them for the underprivileged with whom they wish to identify, and almost a shamefaced attitude is held towards their middle class education and background. There is a desire to improve the human situation and establish a just society.

Again in contrast the House Church Movement will not be concerned with the improvement of this world, but interested in the salvation of souls in preparation for the imminent second coming of Christ.

Perhaps one similarity could be pointed out, and that is in the field of ethics. The radical theologians have welcomed the concepts of situation ethics; although those in the House Churches may not go so far as an explicit acknowledgement such as that, the days of puritanical ethics are gone. There is a more sympathetic consideration of the individual, in applying the biblical standards of morality and ethics with, it is noticed, changes of emphasis in interpreting such standards.

So it can be seen that both theologians and the House Church Movement have made a response to the religious crisis of modern society. Responses which stand in sharp contrast to each other. Parallel to these responses and part of the general process of secularisation has been the decline in the influence of the clergy.

In this country for hundreds of years the cleric enjoyed the privileges of high social rank and being one of the literate few in village communities alongside the local squire. Later they were accorded equal status with members of the medical professions. However, during the fifties and sixties the educational qualifications of ordinands fell, fewer graduates entered orders; between 1960-64 the proportion of non-graduates rose from 50 per cent to over 60 per cent. Similarly the age of entrants rose from 3 per cent over forty years old in 1959 to 12 per cent in 1964.(1) At the same time stipends have not kept pace with inflation so that now the clergy salaries have sunk towards the level of the teaching professions.

The cleric who enters the discussion of radical theology is usually thought odd by the general public who accord scant respect to one who appears to deny what he is paid to uphold. The clergy face their decline in status with different responses.

Some clergy seek satisfaction in social work, others in their pastoral commitments, yet others concentrate on elaborating the liturgy, feeling this is a safe area confined to the specialist. Still others spend their time discussing why their churches are emptying or the relationship between worship and architecture. All try to show they are an indispensable part of society.

The changing role of the clergy can also be related to the changing attitude of society as a whole towards the symbol of authority. The twentieth century has seen the rise of trade unionism with the accompanying emancipation of the working classes, the partial emancipation of women, and a child-centred educational system. All of these have contributed, particularly since the Second World War, to a growing distaste for authoritarian control.

Linked with that was the sudden realisation of the potential of the lay person. Since the dawn of Christianity the priest, then the minister or pastor officiated and the people listened. Now the passive role of the layman is over; since the decade of the fifties the emphasis has been upon an active participation and a renewed interest in the "priesthood of all believers". In the Anglican Church there was talk of the inherent meaning of the role of servant in the title of deacon, so that the church was seen to be run by cooperation between clergy and laymen and no longer with the priesthood the sole prerogative and burden of one man.

In the fifties and sixties the evangelical wing looked to figureheads in mass evangelism such as Billy Graham to bring revival to religious life. Whereas one can cautiously claim a certain degree of success in regard to such campaigns in general the effects of mass evangelism are not permanent. On the whole neither the clergy nor the church are relevant to a vast section of society today. The House Church Movement stands as a reaction against that situation.

The House Church Movement can be clearly seen as an anticlerical movement. In all types there is a common reserve towards the ordained, trained ranks of clerics. In the Harvestime groups particularly the situation of one professional man being in total control of a church, albeit with the help of lay people, is anathema to their concept of church government which must be through a group of men whom they see to be divinely appointed leaders. There is no place for a clergy allied to a hierarchical structure of appointments and clearly associated with the English middle class. Yet it will also be observed that they have in fact instituted a substitute hierarchy of church government.

In every aspect the House Church Movement stands in contrast to the secular society. The house church attempts to create a society of the people of God - in the Harvestime Churches this society is based upon the Old Testament conception of the tribes of Israel, brought by Yahweh into the Promised Land. The House Churches are the tribes who are now entering the Kingdom of God, for the House Church provides not only a fundamentalist theology based upon a literal interpretation of the Bible but an alternative society. A society where God, who is a very personal God, is in control. This God speaks, through words of prophecy given to individuals, he rules through wisdom given to the apostles and elders, and furthermore miracles are expected and experienced, such as the healing of all manner of diseases. It seems as if the House Churches are determined to recreate the type of sacral society from which the secular age is said to have evolved. Members of the church have departed from the secular world into a world controlled by God himself (although they will still work in the "world" they do not consider themselves part of it).

It is interesting to compare the two types of church, the North groups who have tended to become isolated units and the Harvestime who have a wider appeal, continually drawing into their circle neighbours and workmates who are attracted by their lifestyle.

This lifestyle of the House Churches brings God and the Church back into the centre of man's existence. In modern society the Church as an institution has been relegated to the periphery of human experience to be an optional extra rather than the pivot of society. All areas of life that were once under the control of the Church have now passed under the umbrella of the state. The state health services embrace the sick, the aged and the deprived. Education is now the concern of the state, which controls even those schools which retain tenuous religious affiliations. The 1944 Education Act paid lip service to the Christian origins of our education system by stipulating an obligatory assembly and regular religious education classes for all pupils except conscientious objectors. To what extent such a stipulation has been carried out over the past thirty years would be an interesting exercise of research, but it would not be too rash a statement to claim that a generation has grown up largely ignorant of the basic tenets of the Christian faith. The steadily lessening influence of the Church has had a far reaching effect on all sections of society. A National Opinion Poll survey in 1972 provided some interesting indications in twentieth century religious affiliations. Of those who professed strong church connections, i.e. attended church more than once a week, twice as many were in the category of the professional middle classes than in the lower working class group. The percentages themselves (6 per cent in the former against 3 per cent in the latter) show another perhaps more significant factor, that is the low figure of 6 per cent who attend church more than once a week in the middle class grouping. In the same poll 57 per cent of the middle class group said either they never went to church or they did not know how often they attended.(2)

Whereas religious apathy has been customary and expected amongst the working classes, having its roots in the appalling conditions of the industrial towns of the nineteenth century, this apathy has, particularly since the Second World War, infiltrated amongst the professional and middle classes. Once it was considered a mark of middle class respectability to attend church, but now other interests conflict with church loyalty. The increasing mobility of the population in that more families possess more than one car and the establishment of the weekend as of important social significance have both played their part in the decline of church attendance amongst the middle classes. The church has been unable to speak in a clear united voice, to provide realistic solutions to the pressing problems of the day such as the ethical questions of abortion, euthanasia and the fringe elements of society, the drug culture and the drop-outs. This too has contributed to the widespread growth of religious apathy amongst the middle classes.

The House Church is a conscious attempt to rectify the deficiencies of the secular society for it provides not only a place of worship, but shows that man is not the master of his own destiny but perforce must need others with whom to enjoy fellowship as well as God. The House Church is a centre for every activity of the family, in particular close attention is paid to the religious instruction of children and to the relating of their leisure interests to the church environment. The family finds its friends and interests amongst the members of the House Church, so that a secure environment is created which shields the members and particularly the children against the inroads of secularisation.

Whereas the radical theologians are seeking to find out who or what is the basis of truth of all religious claims, and how one can interpret that truth to modern man, those of the House Churches either refuse to see the problems or claim they have solved them by their experiences, for to them God is there, real and personal. Theirs is an experiential theology, which is both traditionally orthodox and uncompromising. They have closed ranks to any suggestion of reinterpretation of doctrine, to any intrusion of the secular, reverting instead to a Davidic type of theocracy.

David Martin has pointed out that revival movements such as the neo-Pentecostalists are in fact a bridge between the old forms of religion and the new. Although the structures might be new, there is a similarity of atmosphere between the new type of worship and old time revivalism; as he puts it, these movements are "filling new forms with old wine".(3)

Certain other trends took place during the fifties and sixties which contributed towards the overall background picture of the religious situation which gave rise to the House Churches. One of these was the attitude towards the religions of the East.

The mid-Victorian desire was to convert the heathen, by the middle of the twentieth century theologians were realising that the Eastern religious thought could perhaps contribute something positive to man's conceptions of the ultimate.

With the continual challenges to tradition Westerners have become less certain that Christianity possesses the only truth, and avenues of compatibility, such as that of meditation, have been explored. There is a freshness and variableness about the Eastern outlook that to the jaded Westerner seems to hold out considerable promise. For instance the Eastern view is of identification with nature rather than the Western attitude of destroying it in the name of progress.(4)

The traditional belief of the Western linear view of history,culminating in the arrival of the Kingdom of God, has been somewhat jolted after the impact of two world wars and a succession of minor troubles and global unrest. Whereas the cyclical view now seems to have more relevance and application to the practicalities of life.

Moreover there is the Eastern attitude towards suffering - which if it does little to achieve its magnitude, at least attempts to explain why such dis-ease in the world exists.

At the very least Eastern influence is bringing a renewed interest in mysticism back into Western religious life.

David Martin described the reaching out of West to East in his definition of a pluralistic society:

> "Tradition is based on a single universe of meaning. Once fracture that universe and its internal harmonics are lost for ever. This is essentially what is meant by pluralism."(5)

Most Protestant radicals and post Vatican II Catholics understand that there are many paths to God.

The House Church Movement is a denial of the pluralistic society and is doggedly affirming the traditions of fundamentalist biblical Christianity which can and does lead to intolerance of other beliefs. The world still exists to be evangelised, although there has as yet been no massive evangelistic outreach, even their mass meetings are geared to the initiated, and evangelism is by personal contact rather than by organised methods. However, those in the House Churches stress that there is only one way to God.

Stephen Neill maintains, "The Age of Missions is at an end, the age of Mission has begun".(6) There has been a completely new transformation of the idea - no longer does the missionary go out to the unknown, to areas unpenetrated by the Gospel. In all probability entry permits would not be granted nowadays, as the Eastern and mid-Eastern religions have closed ranks to what is seen as further Western infiltration. Now the world is smaller, countries no longer live in isolation, with the speed of air communications a commonplace fact of life. The cities of the West are cosmopolitan, full of Moslems, Hindus, Buddhists, whilst the Middle East, India and Japan have a constant stream of businessmen and industrialists from the West. So that the opportunities of mission are there, albeit in very different forms. Probably both at home and abroad the age of preaching has finished, and mission will be by personal one to one contact.

The House Churches were a new development of worship in the decade of the seventies. What is new is often suspect and these churches have no claim for authenticity and no traditions whatever. It is generally agreed that the ideal would be a united Christendom, and that the definitions of denominationalism are wrong. The grouping of Christians under the names of men such as Luther or Calvin or Wesley is all too like the divisions under Apollos or Paul or Cephas (1 Cor. 1:12). The question to be answered is, are the House Churches providing yet another schism or, as they are anxious to maintain, are they demonstrating the coming together of God's people in unity?

From the beginnings of Christianity until the present time there have been wide divergencies of ideas, activities, culture, liturgy and life-style. In New Testament times there were the Hebrews and the Hellenists, the Jewish Christian and the Gentile and as time went on there were the divergencies of East and West, and in the West the split of Catholic and Protestant (with its subsequent divisions).

The Ecumenical Movement historically grew out of the desire for unity, a desire which is as old as the Church itself. In the 19th century concern for unity came from two movements, the Missionary Societies and the Youth Movements such as the Students Christian Movement and the YMCA. Yet whilst acknowledging the contribution the Ecumenical Movement has made it cannot be said to be truly ecumenical whilst large blocks of the Church remain aloof. The Baptist, Roman Catholic and Pentecostal wings still maintain a reserved attitude on points of difference in doctrinal belief.

Hans Küng maintains the concern should be not that there is diversity within the Christian faith but that the divisions should keep lines of contact open with each other and not harden into isolated units.(7)

Of the three types of House Church considered the Harvestime groups have since around 1977 worked to establish good relationships with other churches. The North groups tend to be self contained verging towards iso-lated, possibly this is a reaction to hostility from the denominational churches. From what is known about the Chard groups they tend to be self sufficient and have little contact with other denominations, although their evangelists work in every denominational setting. All cope with criticism and suspicion from Christians in denominational churches, mostly from the evangelical sector; liberals and Catholics tend to be more tolerant, but suspicion and criticism must be counteracted before any kind of relationship can be established.

The importance of Küng's statement cannot be overstressed. Uniformity is practically an impossibility, people are so different temperamentally and culturally. What is needed is a recognition of each other's values as a move towards real spiritual unity.

During the era of the fifties and sixties two very different areas of change came about which deserve closer attention. Firstly the situation in the Roman Catholic Church and secondly the neo-Pentecostal revival, somewhat loosely termed the Charismatic Movement.

For nearly one hundred years the Catholic Church had known internal tensions between modernist and conservative churchmen. Events were to lead up to a decade of the most challenging and far reaching changes since the time of the Reformation - but these changes brought about a radical difference in the papal attitude towards both their own church practices and other Christian denominations.

In 1954 the Vatican stopped the worker priest movement in France - this was the last stamp of the old papal regime. In 1959 John XXIII began his brief but significant reign by immediately calling a second Vatican Council. Social justice and Church unity were his interests and at New Delhi in 1961 for the first time Roman Catholic observers were present at the World Council of Churches.

Vatican II gave the vernacular liturgy to the ordinary Catholics, and the tentative moves towards other churches were begun. These moves were to be on two fronts, on the one the cautious observing of the World Council of Churches and on the other hand the more informal participation in the charismatic meetings organised on an ecumenical basis. Today many Roman Catholic churches have charismatic groups meeting to pray and study the influence of the third person of the Trinity upon the worship of the church. Many such groups work on an ecumenical basis, house masses and what are termed charismatic eucharists are now commonplace and the overall emphasis is one of informal worship.

Bishop Lesslie Newbigin stated in his book "Household of God" that there are three main streams of Christianity. Catholic, Protestant and Pentecostal. This third stream has experienced a phenomenal growth par-ticularly in countries in South America, but also since the sixties, Europe and the USA have seen the progress of the Charismatic Movement. A link between the classic Pentecostalism of the turn of the century,which devel-oped into several independent denominations, and the neo-Pentecostalism of the Charismatic Movement is the work of David du Plessis, who in 1952 met

with leaders of the W.C.C. and later attended the International Missionary
Council at Willengen in Germany.(8) In March 1980 a dialogue took place at
Bossey, Switzerland, between the sub-unit of the World Council of Churches on
Renewal and Congregational Life and members of the Charismatic Renewal, ar-
ranged by the World Council of Churches consultant on Charismatic Renewal,
Dr Arnold Bittlinger.

During the fifties and sixties different individuals began to voice
claims of a Pentecostal experience. Amongst these were an Episcopalian priest
in Van Nuys, California, a Presbyterian minister in Scotland, an Anglican
curate in West London - all unconnected. The year 1963 saw the emergence of
small charismatic groups in several Anglican parishes in England. The individuals concerned were to be consolidated largely through the endeavours of
Michael Harper, who went on to pioneer the work of the Fountain Trust, an
organisation dedicated to promote renewal within the existing denominations.

In 1958 Michael Harper was appointed curate at a well known evangelical
Anglican church, All Souls, Langham Place. Here he met George Ingram, a
retired missionary, whose chief concern was to promote an interest in revival;
to this end he saw it as his duty to constantly remind the staff of All Souls
of the necessity for a second spiritual blessing. Ingram later achieved a
wider circulation for his views in the organisation of monthly Nights of
Prayer for World Revival and his regular newsletter.

On 21-23 September 1962 Michael Harper conducted a weekend conference
at Farnham for a group from St Luke's Church, Hampstead. Whilst preparing
studies on the book of Ephesians for that conference he had an experience of
the Holy Spirit, although at that time he was unsure as to what exactly had
happened. His wife Jeanne had a similar experience on 27th September. They
consulted George Ingram and came to the conclusion this was the second
blessing.

Michael Harper was acquainted with Eric Houfe who introduced him to the
magazine _Trinity_ which was founded and published by Mrs Jean Stone, an
American Episcopelian from Van Nuys, California. This magazine indicated
to the Harpers their new experience was not only individualistic but an
experience for the Church as a whole.

After the weekend at Farnham Michael Harper began to receive invitations
to speak on the subject of the Holy Spirit.   One was to St Mark's Church,
Gillingham in Kent, where the incumbent, the Revd John Collins, was a former
curate of All Souls, Langham Place. Early in 1963 Michael Harper preached at
St Mark's; following his visit the church met for a night of prayer on 1st
February 1963. During the night a number of the congregation were baptised
in the Spirit. Two former curates of St Mark's have since become well known
in charismatic circles: David Watson in connection with St Michael's, York,
and David McInnes in Birmingham.

At St Mark's, Michael Harper had met Barry Sillitoe who was serving in
the army but originated from Burslem, near Stoke on Trent.   What he said
caused Michael Harper to begin a correspondence with the Rector of Burslem,
Philip L.C. Smith.

Philip Smith and his wife Norah had become interested in the Pentecostal experience when two young members of their youth group, Ron Bailey and his girlfriend Margaret, claimed to have been baptised in the Holy Spirit through the influence of Pentecostal friends. (Ron and Margaret Bailey are now leaders of a house church in Moseley, Birmingham which is associated with Mr. G.W. North.) On 28th September 1962 Ron and Margaret prayed for the Smiths and they too entered into the experience. In May 1963 Michael Harper invited clergy he thought would be sympathetic to hear Frank Macguire from California speak. Macguire recommended Larry Christenson as another speaker; he visited London later that year.

Early in August 1963 the Harpers and Smiths met in Cambridge and prayed together. By that time the Harpers were interested in speaking in tongues. Philip Smith visited All Souls later that week and prayed with the other curate Martin Peppiatt, who has since been active in charismatic renewal, and George Forester, vicar of St Paul's Beckenham.

Later in August a young American Lutheran, Larry Christenson, was in England. Michael Harper invited clergy and full-time church workers to a meeting at which Christenson spoke. It was at that time that Christenson advised Michael Harper to try to speak in tongues. From that time the differences between Harper and his vicar John Stott grew wider. The next meeting Harper arranged was not on the premises of All Souls but at the Londoner Hotel when David du Plessis was the speaker in October 1963.

Meanwhile another centre of Pentecostal activity was St Paul's Church, Beckenham in Kent. George Forester, the vicar, had received the Baptism in the Spirit through the ministry of Richard Bolt, a Pentecostal minister now associated with the church at South Chard. Meetings held in the vicarage caused widespread interest in the locality. Different Pentecostal speakers were invited; one of these (Reimer de Graaf, a Dutchman) was a close friend of Goos Vedder, a minister of the Harvestime group of house churches. The situation at St Paul's was tense,and eventually George Forester resigned over the issue of infant baptism and subsequently became a pastor in an Assembly of God church.

The events at Beckenham were given extensive coverage in the Church of England Newspaper, and from this time religious press reports provided an important vehicle for publicising the progress of charismatic renewal. Michael Harper contributed to the ensuing debate in the press and thus became known as a pioneer in what was now seen as a definite movement in the church. The movement spread through three areas of communication: personal correspondence, conferences, which were always recorded so that tapes and cassettes brought the message to an increasingly wider circle, and literature. An account was opened by business friends to fund the meetings arranged, and in January 1964 Michael Harper began a newsletter which was at first issued bimonthly, then monthly.

On 16th February 1964 the first conference took place at Stoke Poges; Campbell MacAlpine was the speaker. In June 1964 Michael Harper left All Souls, as his prime interest now lay in promoting the Charismatic Movement. A charitable trust was set up which was to be known as the Fountain Trust; the aim was to renew the church, not divide it, so that this was not to be an organisation that anyone could join. Michael Harper was appointed director at the beginning of July. The previous month David du Plessis and the Harpers toured England and Scotland, holding twenty five meetings which served as a launching for the Fountain Trust.

Interest was aroused in the Church, and in January 1964 the Charismatic Movement was debated at the Islington clerical conference with the largest ever attendance. It was also the subject for discussion at the annual Baptist Revival Fellowship Conference in November of the same year, and Michael Harper spoke at the Southport Evangelical Conference of clergy and church workers of northern dioceses. This was still seen as a phenomenon within the evangelical sector of the Church and certain notable evangelicals such as John Stott, Alan Stibbs and Jim Packer, had spoken out strongly against the movement. The classic Pentecostals too were also suspicious of a Pentecostalism which remained in the historic churches; George Canty of the British Pentecostal Fellowship voiced these suspicions in an article in The Ministry (October/December 1964).

A considerable lift was given to the charismatic cause in November 1965 by the arrival at the London Hilton of the American Pentecostal Full Gospel Businessmen's Fellowship International who stayed for two weeks. The encouragement of such a successful male contingent gave the English Charismatics fresh vigour.

The Charismatic Movement can be seen as emerging in different strands, many working for renewal within the denominational churches. Such a strand is the Full Gospel Businessmen's Fellowship International (FGBMFI).(9) The literal vision in 1953 of an American Armenian Pentecostal, Demos Shakarian, was of men all over the world coming alive to praise God. This group is not a church but an association of businessmen who convene breakfast meetings, luncheons or dinners and also residential conferences. These meetings always have the same form, that of testimonies, never preaching. Prominent businessmen are invited to tell their personal stories, how God has worked in their lives and how their faith has developed. The FGBMFI transcends all denominations and works to revitalise all churches. It is noteworthy that Demos Shakarian had a vision of men praising God. This was no accident; for some years he had felt keenly the lack of male support in the American Pentecostal churches, which was so foreign to his own Armenian culture. In a very similar way to the leaders of the House Churches, he felt the need to restore male influence in the churches.

Also in 1965 it became known that the movement was not restricted to evangelicals. Two brothers, Michael Meakin and A.R. Meakin, both clerics, though not evangelical, exercised a charismatic ministry in their respective churches at Woburn Sands and Emmanuel Church, Loughborough. They had both attended the First Conference at Stoke Poges in 1964.

The official magazine of the Fountain Trust, Renewal, began its bi-monthly publication in January 1966.

After 1967 the Roman Catholic interest in the Charismatic Movement became apparent, causing the suspicions to mount in evangelical and Pentecostal circles at the dangerous tendency of the charismatics to place experience above the fundamental truths of biblical Protestantism. Then in May 1969 at the Fountain Trust Conference at High Leigh there was a significantly large conference contingent from Anglo-Catholic backgrounds. When Michael

Harper visited the United States in 1969 he met Catholic Charismatics, whose influence was to shape the future direction of the Fountain Trust in England. The next meeting in November 1969 was held on the theme of Catholic Pentecostalism.

The vision grew that the Charismatic Movement was for every sector of the Church in every part of the world. The first International Conference was held at Guildford in 1971, which proved to be the culmination of the early history of the movement. Henceforth the charismatic renewal achieved a wider recognition in all denominations and commanded a respect hitherto unknown.

The first Methodist Charismatic Conference in 1973 for one hundred and thirty five delegates was reviewed in the Methodist Recorder. The Methodist Conference of 1974 endorsed a report on the movement which praised charismatics for "a patient acceptance of the Spirit's influence". But the Methodist leaders were concerned that the numbers of students in the Bible Colleges were disproportionately charismatic. The United Reformed Church now has a group for Evangelism and Renewal which is led by charismatics. The Roman Catholic Church set up a National Service Centre for Catholic Charismatic Renewal. The British Council of Churches published a theological enquiry, Can the Pentecostal Movement Renew the Churches?, written by a Roman Catholic, Emmanuel Sullivan. In the meantime local Fountain Trust meetings sprang up all over the country. On the tenth anniversary of the Fountain Trust the magazine Renewal contained messages of appreciation from the Archbishop of Canterbury, Lord Macleod and the General Secretary of the British Council of Churches.

Papal endorsement of the Roman Catholic charismatic renewal came at a conference of 10,000 delegates in Rome in May 1975. Michael Harper had played a prominent part in the Catholic/Pentecostal dialogues which had been held once a year since 1972.(10) Some evangelicals saw these meetings as a threat from Rome to make a take over bid for the Anglican Church, and certainly the Fountain Trust appears to have achieved greater measure of success with those of Catholic sympathies than with those in the free churches.

Tom Smail joined the Fountain Trust as secretary in 1972 and succeeded Michael Harper as its director in 1975. Harper went on to a position as curate in a West London parish whilst at the same time continuing to write and to travel. After four years as director Tom Smail took a teaching appointment at St John's Theological College, Nottingham, in September 1979. The new director was an Anglican cleric, Michael Barling.

Many of those concerned with the Charismatic Movement asked the question: Where Now? In the June/July 1979 issue of Renewal (11) Tom Smail wrote,

> "I believe that as an exclusive party we have no future that matters, but the time has come for the charismatic movement to stop being a thing in itself, to ally itself with all other movements for renewal that are also, for all their limitations and fallibility, signs that God is alive and at work in his Church."

The work of the Fountain Trust finally came to an end on the 31st December, 1980.

Maybe the Charismatic Movement will eventually cease to be a distinctive force. In considering the formation and progress of the House Church Movement the difference of emphasis becomes very apparent, which difference can only result in the House Churches becoming more exclusive and sectarian.

At first glance it would be easy to see the House Churches emerging as part of the main Charismatic Movement. Those involved in the House Churches believe that their task began at an independent point. Neither Mr G.W. North, nor the founders of the Harvestime Churches, nor the leaders of the Church at South Chard had any connection with the Fountain Trust movement of renewal in the denominations. Each had their own ideas as to what the church should be and the way in which renewal should evolve.

It can be seen that in a world threatened by insecurity politically and internationally, the House Church Movement represents in one way a step back - into a secure environment which is supernaturally controlled, and in another way it is a step forward - into what they see as the eschatological grouping of the people of God.

The Charismatic Movement of the late fifties and sixties resulted in various expressions of religious phenomena; one of these is the movement loosely termed House Churches. It must be said at the outset that, although these began as meetings in houses, many have now expanded into larger premises, such as school halls and disused churches.

The three main types of House Church which are to be found in this country will be seen to have originated quite independently of each other and of the main stream of the Charismatic Movement. Nevertheless, their ranks have been considerably swelled by those known as "Charismatics" who have left the denominational churches.

The essential nature of the Charismatic Movement which emphasised the activity of the third person of the Trinity gave rise to an immediate division in the local church situation, into those who had entered into a new experience, and those who had not. Reactions to that situation resulted in one or other of two sequels. Either the majority of members in a church enthusiastically sought this new experience and the whole life and character of the church changed, or the members of the church split into two groups, those who had had an experience of the Holy Spirit and those who had not. In that case, future developments in the life of the church depended upon the attitude of the minister and/or those in positions of authority such as the elders, deacons, or oversight. Where those in authority were favourably disposed towards the new experience, those who were not interested were often made to feel like second class citizens. This resulted in a lack of harmony so that some even left to find a place of worship more congenial.

Where those in authority were suspicious of the claims of the new Pentecostals the latter began to seek opportunity to meet together to enjoy their newly discovered forms of worship. Many ecumenical types of house meetings have sprung up whose members still retain their allegiance to the denominational churches. But from this move of people wishing to worship in a new way has arisen the growth of groups or chains of House Churches. Such people felt a dissatisfaction, not only with worship but with the whole tenor of church life.

Of two main chains of fellowships to be considered the first is a group I shall refer to, for purposes of identification, as Harvestime. The second are those fellowships which have arisen from the work of a Mr G.W. North. A third influence comes from an independent Pentecostal Church in Somerset. My information on this last group is very sparse as the founders and leaders did not wish the history and work of their church to be included in this study. Accordingly it was very difficult to obtain any first hand information. I am greatly indebted to Mr Andrew Jordan, one of the Elders, who sent me a brief resume of the origins of the work, and I hope that through ignorance I shall not make any inaccurate comments.

An important point to note is that no group of churches wishes to be known under any common title. Each simply has a local name. This is a reaction to the bitter accusation from denominational churches that house churches are causing a further fragmentation of the body of Christ and are thus creating a new denomination. All stress that they have no name and no central organisation and therefore they cannot be denominations.

The Harvestime Churches

The first group to be considered, those I call the Harvestime Churches, began as a church in a house, and although many of these have now outgrown this definition they are still spoken of as the House Church Movement, a term they themselves do not care for. The rapid growth of these "churches in houses" as they prefer to be called has led to the transference of the meeting places to hired halls, often school halls which are available for Sunday meetings.

The leaders of the movement are adamant that they are not a denomination, and in this statement is the key to their basic concept of the church. They maintain that denominations have fragmented the Church of God, that each revival in history has produced more fragmentations, but that now God is beginning to work in a new way in that He is calling out and uniting people of all denominations. These people are worshipping and living together in closely related groups, whilst maintaining the family unit. At the beginning of the decade of the eighties they numbered between 35,000 and 40,000 in this country, and these fellowships have continued to increase.

The emphasis of the movement lies in the concept of the Church. The question is posed - "Are denominations right?" If they are, there is no problem; if not, then they should cease. To the question that they themselves must be forming a denomination is given the reply that a denomination must have a central governing body, whereas the only link between their churches is the Apostolic and Prophetic ministry which is exercised by those leaders (from many different places) moving and travelling around among the churches. There is no central Headquarters, they maintain.

The whole concept of a new form of church structure arose some years ago out of the discussions of a group of men at the start of the decade of the sixties. Amongst that group was Bryn Jones who with his younger brother Keri was the formative influence of the Harvestime Churches.

Bryn Jones was born in 1939, his brother Keri in 1944, a sister Doreen was born in 1942. The family lived in the mining community of Aberdare; their mother was an Anglican, their father held no Christian belief. Both brothers felt the deepest influence on their early lives was a mother who prayed. They are proud of their working class background; both had to leave school to go to work as soon as the "O" level examinations had been taken.

Aberdare had been one of the centres of the Welsh revival of 1904, and the churches in the district were those which came out of that spiritual movement. Consequently there was much talk in the communities of the experiences of former years, how hundreds flocked to chapel, and men deserted the pubs to hear the gospel message.

24

In 1957 Bryn Jones had a conversion experience; he became known amongst local church people as an earnest evangelical, enthusiastic to uphold the authority of scripture and very much opposed to Pentecostal ideas. In 1958 a man called William Hartley came to preach at the local Assemblies of God Pentecostal Church. William Hartley was known to have a ministry of healing. One evening Bryn Jones went to a healing meeting with the intention to denounce Hartley for preaching error, which he did. The curious fact was that inexplicably he returned to the meeting the following evening, where he experienced the Pentecostal "Baptism in the Spirit" and thereafter joined the Assemblies of God Church. From the beginning Bryn Jones seems to have had a "successful" ministry (his adjective would probably be "blessed"). He was greatly influenced by Rhys Howell's teaching on the life of faith in his book "Intercessor" and so he went to the Bible College of Wales at Swansea. After completing the course there he went to Cornwall with a colleague, Robert Hislop, who is now a missionary to the Iboe tribe in Nigeria, and still linked to Harvestime. During this time in Cornwall they practised the principles of living by faith, without any sources of income. They often went without food; their diet consisted largely of mushrooms picked in the early morning. Whilst in Cornwall they saw certain religious phenomena occur at the Methodist church at St Austell, where individuals professed to be healed of various ills and many claimed to have received the Baptism in the Spirit. This claim to a miracle content appears to be a feature of Bryn Jones's public ministry.

From Cornwall Bryn Jones moved to Germany and then to France, where he worked for three months with Operation Mobilisation, an International Youth Mission. It was there he met his wife, Edna Williams, who shared his interest in a Pentecostal type ministry. The following year in May 1964 they were married and left for Guyana in South America, where they worked as missionaries for three years. Bryn Jones established twenty-seven churches during those three years. At present there are sixty churches in that area, all linked with the Harvestime Churches in England.

Meanwhile his younger brother, Keri, was preparing for a similar work. Keri had known a conversion experience in 1958, the year after his brother, and had received the Baptism in the Spirit three years later in 1961. In 1963 Keri also went to the Bible College of Wales, where he met Goos Vedder, a young Dutchman, who was to become a close colleague in the Harvestime movement.

When Bryn and Edna Jones returned home to England they travelled back by way of the United States. On that return journey they met Robert Ewing, from Waco, Texas. He was connected to a church which had come from the Latter Rain Movement. This Robert Ewing was to be the first connection the Harvestime Churches had with churches in America.

On returning to England Bryn decided to resume his work in Cornwall, his brother joined him, and they endeavoured to establish churches. From the outset this was a very difficult period, not because of antagonism or apathy, but because of the quarrelling factions in that area who were constantly squabbling about points of church practice. These squabbles centred around the rite of adult baptism. Some of the Christian groups, notably the church at South Chard, at that time were baptising converts, not in the formula of the Trinity, but in the name of Jesus. Difficulties arose when the advocates of this began to rebaptise people, telling them that their former baptism in the name of the Trinity was not valid. Much bad feeling was caused. The Jones brothers refused to take sides in the dispute and eventually felt the wisest course would be to leave the area.

So in 1968 Bryn Jones went to Bradford and Keri Jones went to a college of education to train for teaching. He married Carol Sexton the following year in 1969.

In Bradford Bryn Jones was asked to be the temporary pastor of a church known as the New Covenant Church. This was an independent church which had been largely established by Mr G.W. North. After six months Mr North sent a permanent pastor, Peter Paris, to the church. Subsequently Peter Paris began to work closely with Bryn Jones, and that particular church relinquished the leadership of Mr North and Bradford became the starting point of the Harvestime Churches.

The work began to expand in 1970, when the first of the summer camps was held, in a field at Pendine, South Wales. Two marquees, one for meetings, the other for eating, a team of three volunteer cooks and a set of tents for hire to would-be campers were the total equipment. The idea was to provide a holiday, with Christian speakers in the mornings and evenings. The following two years this camp was repeated with the addition of a short Bible school held a few weeks later.

During this time it was realised that there was a need for Christians in all denominations and all walks of life to come together in closer unity. By this time Bryn Jones had come to know men in the Full Gospel Businessmen's Fellowship International and also Sir Thomas and Lady Faith Lees of Post Green near Poole. It became obvious that the miner's sons had much in common with the titled gentry and this was felt to be significantly pointing the way to further development in the concept of a church, unhindered by the trappings of denomination, tradition or social status.

Another group of men began to meet for further discussions and prayer. Bryn Jones and Arthur Wallis from the first group together with Graham Perrins, John Noble, Peter Line, John McClaughlin and Barney Coombs. It was significant that each of these men had a church in their home, and from this grew the name the House Church Movement. People saw this as the start of a new denomination.

Their discussions centred on the prophetic teaching of the Scriptures, basically the teaching on Israel and eschatology. They believed at that time that these meetings would develop into a greater significance than a gathering together to study the Bible.

During the times of fasting, prayer and studying together there emerged among them those with the ministries of apostles, prophets, pastors and teachers, which was the beginning of a nationwide movement of related fellowships. They were however conscious that this structure of authority based on Paul's teaching in 1 Corinthians 12 was not new. At the time of the Welsh Revival in 1904 a pastor, Don Williams, saw clearly the role of the apostolic and prophetic ministry, and on that basis founded the Apostolic Church. The tragedy of that church was that it became too insular and exclusive, so with that in mind the Harvestime Churches are anxious to maintain connections with those in the denominational churches, recognising that men other than those in their own groups may possess a prophetic ministry.

In 1971 Bryn Jones received the first invitation to go to the United States. The man Robert Ewing whom he had met on his return journey from Guyana in 1966 invited him to speak at a convention in Waco, Texas. He gave Bryn Jones the name of the church in Goshen, Indiana, where he would be met and taken to the Convention. This church met in a shop. Bryn and his brother Keri planned to stay one night before they moved on. The night he arrived Bryn Jones was asked to speak. During the meeting so many people were helped through his ministry, many claiming to have received healing, that he was asked to stay longer than the one night that had been arranged.

One night Bryn Jones received a vision of the next church he was intended to visit. The vision took place during the night but was described not as a dream but rather as a mental picture. A church was seen which had a steeple and a bell. The door and the windows were painted red.

When the time came for them to go on to the Convention Robert Ewing arrived. He suggested that on the way to Waco they called at his home church in St Louis, Missouri. This was a church which met in an old fire station. At the meeting there were thirty-two people of whom eight were visiting ministers. When the time came for the collection to be taken Bryn Jones was interested to see that the collecting box was in the shape of a church, the design of which was identical to the church he had seen in his mental picture whilst lying awake the previous night. This he felt was the church where he should stay for a while and work.

He went on to the Convention, where his preaching was appreciated, and where again many people claimed to have experienced miracles of healing. Then he returned to St Louis - today the church there numbers 4,500 people, who regard Bryn Jones as the Apostle who established the church.

Subsequently to that visit Bryn Jones and some of his colleagues have visited the States many times working in towns from Waco, Texas to St Louis, Missouri and in Valparaiso, Indiana. Many new churches have been started. In the summer of 1978 Peter Paris and his family moved to Little Rock, Arkansas, to work in the church there.

Back in England the summer camps continued at Amney Crucis near Cirencester in the grounds of a private estate in 1973 and at Post Green in 1974. Now there was an explicit teaching on the necessity for authority in the church coupled with a strong emphasis on authority in the family.

Then in 1973 Bryn Jones was asked to speak at the annual Convention, held at Capel, the Bible College of the Elim Church. This Convention was organised by a committee of men of all denominations; one was Barney Coombs, minister of an independent Baptist church at Basingstoke, others were Harold Owen and Gerald Coates, all of whom subsequently became part of the Harvestime Churches.

In 1974 an American Ern Baxter was asked to speak at Capel; he shared the platform with Bryn Jones. When the two met they realised that during his visit to the States in 1971 Bryn Jones had visited many churches with whom

Ern Baxter had direct links, and straightaway a mutual sympathy was felt. Following that Capel Convention Bryn Jones invited Ern Baxter to be the principal speaker at the next summer camp. This was to be a significant step forward in the development of the movement. The camp had now grown from around 50 to 2,000 people, the majority of whom camped in the grounds of a conference centre in the Lake District, known as Blaithwaite House.

The message of the speaker, Ern Baxter, initiated the formation of many small independent groups into the closely linked body of churches that exist today. The theme of his message was the Government of God - the teaching was done entirely by allegory - showing a clear distinction between the democratic appointments of the denominational churches, as illustrated in the Old Testament by the democratic election of King Saul, and the divine appointment of God now being seen in the new House Churches and illustrated by the divine choice of King David. From that time onward many leaders of local groups contacted the organisers of the convention and entered into a firm relationship with them. The following year, in 1976, a larger venue was found in the Agricultural Showground at Harrogate, where the numbers increased each year until in 1978 they reached 8,000 residents on site plus some considerable numbers of day visitors. This number was maintained over the next few years. This Annual Conference is known as the Dales Bible Week.

Following the growth of the friendship between Ern Baxter and Bryn Jones the links between the churches in England and those of like persuasion in the States grew. It is stressed that these links are entirely personal and not governmental. There is no administrative connection at all, but many instances of Apostles and Elders crossing the Atlantic to visit and preach in each other's churches and areas. Dr Ern Baxter introduced his colleagues, Bob Mumford, Derek Prince and Charles Simpson. They in turn introduced others, Larry Christenson, Ralph Martin and Kevin Ranaghan, to the English leaders. These were from different denominational backgrounds, the last two named from the Roman Catholic Church.

The influence of the Harvestime Churches has extended in other directions. In Norway a man called Erling Thui heard of Bryn Jones and in 1975 wrote to ask him to visit Norway. When Bryn Jones and David Mansell arrived in Norway they met a leading Pentecostal minister, Tom Erlandson of Stavanger Assemblies of God Church. Tom Erlandson re-structured his church on the lines advocated by the Harvestime Churches.

In Spain a Protestant evangelist, Samuel de Cosa, who works amongst the Spanish gypsies, began to receive opportunities to preach in Roman Catholic communities. He saw a copy of the Harvestime magazine Restoration and wrote asking if it would be possible for the magazine to be translated into Spanish. In 1976 Terry Virgo was sent out to Spain, with David Tomlinson, Michael Stevens (an ex-major of the British army) and David Mansell. These leaders worked with Samuel de Cosa, and the following summer he together with a Catholic priest came to the Dales Bible Week at Harrogate, where the latter spoke about his work at Calpe in Southern Spain.

In 1975 Ted Kent, a prominent member of the English branch of the FGBMFI, and a close friend of Bryn Jones, went to live in Kenya. He joined an all black Kenyan church. It is believed he was the first white man to do that.

In 1977 he asked Bryn Jones and David Mansell to visit Kenya. There they pioneered a new church at Thika, and they also had opportunity to speak to some government officials. (There has been some considerable Christian influence in the Kenyan government in that many of the officials were educated at the Alliance High School.)

In 1978 the two paid a return visit; shortly before they left England, during the Convention that was held at Harrogate, they were told in a word of prophecy that they would have an opportunity to speak with high officials in Kenya. On this second visit Jomo Kenyatta died, and just prior to his death he summoned all the white missionaries together to ask them, "Why is it when I am trying to unite the tribes, are you white missionaries trying to undo my efforts by presenting a Christianity which is divisive?"

After Kenyatta's death the nation was called to prayer. Bryn Jones and David Mansell were invited to meet the new President, Arap Moi, an evangelical Christian. They spoke to him for over an hour about the Kingdom of God. He gave permission for the magazine Restoration to be brought into the country and promised to write a foreword and allow his photograph to be on the front cover of the first issue. Since that time the President meets each month with Harry Das, who is one of the Apostles of the Harvestime Churches, a South American who became a Christian under the ministry of Bryn Jones, and who works in Kenya on behalf of the Harvestime Churches.

During that visit the two leaders saw many miracles of healing occur in the black churches in which they preached. The fellowships in England then sponsored a Windmill project, that is every £5,000 raised bought a water mill for a Kenyan tribe in an effort to make them self supporting. Land has also been bought and given to the tribes people. Plans were made for teachers from the Bradford church to go out to work in the Kenyan government schools and black churches.

During 1977 some of the leaders such as Arthur Wallis, Peter Paris, Alan Vincent, Hugh Tomlinson, went out to India to conduct seminars. They travelled, visiting Bombay, Kashmir and Udhampur. It is now planned that copies of Restoration will be translated into the Indian dialects and sent out in the near future.

In the Argentine, Bryn Jones, David Mansell, and David Tomlinson worked with an evangelist, Orvil Swindol, for three months.

In South Africa a minister in Natal, Pieter Maritzburg, heard through an Australian friend, Howard Carter (a friend of Ern Baxter), about the development of the churches in England. He and a colleague came to England in 1977 and stayed for a week in Bradford visiting the church. In 1978 they returned bringing their whole church group to the Convention at Harrogate. Now there are hopes that the magazine Restoration will be translated into local dialects for the coloured Christians in Natal.

Bryn Jones, his wife and family left in October 1978 for the New Covenant church of St Louis, Missouri, where they have worked with the minister Bob Beckett. They returned to England briefly in April 1979 for the International Conference for leaders which took place in Bradford over a period of six weeks, and have subsequently returned for the annual conferences at Harrogate.

The administrative quarters for the annual conventions, the bookshop, and the extensive tape and cassette recording, and sales department, of both speakers and religious musical groups is The Church House, Bradford. A further publishing house issues the bi-monthly magazine and other books.

Church House was the former Anglican diocesan headquarters; when church finances could not maintain the vast Victorian building, Bryn Jones and his associates bought it. Collections raised part of the purchase price and on the rest a mortgage was raised. When bought in January 1977 it was in a delapidated condition; over the next two years it was completely redesigned internally and refurbished.

In conclusion the Harvestime Churches have experienced a meteoric growth from 1975, and their influence is also reaching out to other countries. The undoubted enthusiasm and dedicated lifestyle of the founders of the Harvestime Churches is unquestionable. However, the rise of these churches occasions some surprise. I see the reasons for such a phenomenon to lie in two areas.

Firstly, this growth is no accident. Bryn Jones and his close colleagues obviously intended to begin a work which would have a wider impact than that of the average evangelist. There is seen a definite aim to establish related churches, whilst at the same time denying the creation of a new schism.

Secondly it is noticed that the movement as such gained impetus after the American connection was established, and in particular after Dr Ern Baxter spoke at the annual Conference in 1975. In effect the latter launched the movement into a chain of rapidly expanding churches. American influence in church life has been noticed before; the Billy Graham Crusades of the fifties and sixties gave an uplift to the evangelical areas of the English Church. A very striking feature of these churches is that all appear to be financially secure. The giving of the church members is on a scale not seen in the historic denominations; most churches either lease or own a bookshop where profits accrue not from the religious books but from the wide range of other goods which are stocked. These churches have benefited from American ideas of financial management and administration.

It will be interesting to see future development, whether the growth has now reached its peak and numbers will stabilise, and the concentration turn to interior developments; or whether these churches will continue to attract large numbers of new members.(1)

The North Churches

This second group of churches is distinct from the former in that they stem from the work of one man rather than a group. Mr G.W. North had no formal theological training. At the close of the Second World War he owned a timber business at Plaxtol in Kent which dealt in different types of fencing and stakes. In his spare time he would preach in different churches in the area.

During 1946 he was invited to preach in an independent Baptist church at Loose, near Maidstone, and subsequently he was asked to take on the pastorate. Accordingly he left his business and became a full time pastor. He stayed at

Loose for six years, after which he received the invitation to become the pastor of a small Holiness church in Bradford.

The period that Mr North spent at Bradford, from 1952-65, appears to have been a dramatic one in the life of the church, and one which signalled the future development of his ministry. He himself emphasises the role of prayer in the life of the church at that time; as he said, "All that happened was born in prayer, and continued in prayer". Parallel with that major role of prayer was the importance given to the exposition of the Bible.

The life of the church began to expand, there were open air services and door to door visitation. They began to hold late night meetings on Saturday evenings for drunks, they sent out teams to visit public houses, clubs and dance halls. Mr North claimed that during that time "the church saw drug addicts, alcoholics and those demon possessed made free and new people when they were delivered by the power of God". The church grew in numbers, and Mr North looks back to this time as a period when he himself learnt a great deal.

Towards the end of thirteen years in Bradford Mr North received an invitation from the trustees of a house on the Wirral in Cheshire, called The Longcroft. The Longcroft had been built as a family home in the twenties by the Milner family who manufactured safes. When the husband died the widow divided the inheritance and the daughter Mary received the house. She gave it back to her mother to use for preventative and rehabilitative work in cases of mental stress. The trustees wanted Mr North to be the chaplain of the house.

In 1965 he moved to The Longcroft, and opportunities opened up for him to preach at other places in the city of Liverpool. There was a regular mid-week meeting at the Friends Meeting House, Harmer Street; this began to expand. On Sunday afternoons a Bible study was held in a house in one of the poorest districts in the city - Liverpool 8. This was mainly for young people; as the numbers grew an additional meeting was started on Tuesday evenings. Presently it became obvious that the house was too small as people were crowded into two upstairs rooms, the landing and the stairs, both upward and downward flights.

The next step was to buy a bigger house, so in 1966 steps were taken to acquire 14, Devonshire Road, Princes Park. It was scheduled for demolition as the area was undergoing redevelopment. It was on the market for £4,000 and enquirers were told this sum would easily be recouped on rents during the time before demolition was due.

A small group of four - Mr North, Norman Meaton, one of the trustees of The Longcroft, David Weatherley and Mrs Jean Porter - met to pray about the proposed purchase. As they had no money at all they decided to ask God for a miracle. They decided they should offer half the asking price - £2,000. Their prayer was: "Lord, we want that house for £2,000, not a penny more or less."

Norman Meaton went to see the agent who represented the property owner in London. His answer was that they would never obtain it for so low a figure - but the following day there was a phone call for him to say the

31

owner had sent a message, for no apparent reason, to say the purchase price of the house could be lowered to £2,000. The group understood this to be a miracle.

They still had no money. The day afterwards one individual sent £1,000 as a gift, and shortly afterwards a second offered £1,000 on loan. The house was in good condition. It has not been demolished and in the early eighties was still in regular use, and accommodated 200 people at a meeting.

The meetings held in that house were characterised by the varied cross section of people who came, from University students to the "scouses" who were ignorant of their parentage, but all wanted to study the Bible. Gradually visitors began to come from further afield; these were people disillusioned with the denominational churches. They would return home with the intention of starting a similar meeting, and as these new groups came into being Mr North would be invited to go to speak to them. It was at this point that these house churches began to spring up in different parts of the country. There is however no organisation which links these fellowships - each is completely autonomous. The only link is the ministry of Mr North and other preachers such as Norman Meaton. Mr North is at pains to emphasise it is always an invited ministry.

It was during a conference in August 1968 that the trustees of The Longcroft suggested to Mr North that they felt they would be selfish if they did not release him to a wider ministry. He said they would discuss and pray about it later and by September he had decided to leave. On the last day of the year he left Liverpool for Exeter. He chose Exeter because in a prayer meeting David Weatherley had spoken a word of prophecy which said.

> "The heart of the King is in the hands of the Lord. He turneth it withersoever he will as the streams of the south."

From that he knew that me must go south.

At Exeter a small fellowship existed. Mr North chose Exeter as a base for an itinerant ministry, he was not the pastor. However, the small group benefited from his ministry and they began to increase, eventually buying a derelict chapel for their meeting place.

The first invitation to preach abroad came from a contact in the Bethany fellowship (a missionary society). A member of that society was visiting a Conference Centre in Minneapolis, USA, when he was asked if he knew any suitable speakers. He gave Mr North's name. The first invitation came in 1969 to the States, since then Mr North states "a world-wide ministry has developed".

As he began to travel abroad more frequently he considered another move. It was obvious that the climate of the West Country did not suit him, also it would be more convenient if he and his family lived closer to an international air terminal. He thought of moving closer to Heathrow.

Then when speaking at a Conference in Liverpool he heard about the purchase of a house in Auchenheath. Dr J.C.C. Kelly, a consultant heart physician at Paisley Infirmary, had held meetings in his home in Glasgow for some

years, although always outside times of church services, so as not to detract
worshippers. He had now bought a house at Auchenheath standing in twenty-five
acres of grounds. His wife attended the Conference in Liverpool and later
Mr North was invited to Auchenheath to speak to the fellowship. Thereafter
regular invitations followed and they became firm friends. At the same time
Mr North was "waiting on the Lord" to see where he should live. He began to
consider Scotland; when he telephoned the Kelly's to say "God had laid
Auchenheath on his heart" they were delighted.

Dr and Mrs Kelly prepared a home for Mr North and his wife in The Lodge
at the gates of the estate. Auchenheath is twenty miles from Prestwick where
there is an international airport and twenty miles from Glasgow which has a
commuter airport. Now Mr North's work is entirely of an itinerant nature;
he travels in the British Isles, Europe, the Mediterranean countries,
Canada, the USA, India and the Nepal. Invitations from all parts of the
world come, many of which he can never fulfil. From this has grown other
work such as that of Norman Meaton of Liverpool and Derek Gitsham of
Worcester.

Mr North sees the present growth of house churches as a fulfilment of
the prophecies spoken by George Jeffreys, the founder of the Elim Four
Square Gospel Church and Smith Wigglesworth, one of the earliest influences
in the Assemblies of God Church. Both prophesied, Wigglesworth when in
Australia, that the next move of the Spirit of God would spring up in homes,
which would be like little lights shining across the land.

Mr North denies emphatically that he intends to initiate a new denomination or even encourage one to develop - in fact, he points out he has never
actually started a house church, but that each situation into which he has
been called has already consisted of a group, so that his ministry has been
one of encouragement rather than initiation.

At a meeting held for four hundred men in Birmingham on 21st April 1979
he stated:

> "I have no wish or desire that any kind of denomination should
> develop and so far as I am concerned to the best of my ability
> it never will. What others do when the Lord takes me is not
> my business, it is my wish that the house fellowships should
> remain completely autonomous, with no central government or
> organisation or denomination or standing or name. I person-
> ally have no powers over any, I go in various fellowships
> only by invitation. It is however impossible to fulfil all
> the invitations I receive."

He further expressed the view that the vision dies with the man. He
quoted the case of General Booth and the way the Salvation Army made the
decision to consolidate rather than expand after the death of the General
and so lost the spiritual vision of its founder and crystallised its activities into social work.

His view is that in each generation God starts something new - in every
generation God raises up men with a fresh vision. When asked what he felt
would happen to the house fellowships after his death, he replied that they

33

would either fade away, or their leaders would crystallise them into another denomination, but that was not his wish.(2)

These fellowships have not the appeal of the Harvestime groups. Despite his attempts to show the contrary it seems obvious that this group of house fellowships stems from the influence of one man, G.W. North. He maintains his work has been to encourage rather than to initiate churches. Nevertheless the fellowships bear remarkable resemblances to each other, both in the style of worship and in such instances as the wearing of a three cornered headscarf by the women during the meeting. His personality has undoubtedly influenced others of leadership calibre and it is noticeable that some of his personal mannerisms, phraseology and preaching techniques have been adopted by such leaders, which fact appears to pass unnoticed by rank and file members. As Mr North travels around the fellowships he is shown respect amounting almost to reverence by members.

Mr North was very vague about any enumeration of the fellowships. He mentioned fellowships in Surrey, Berkshire, the West Country, the Midlands, Yorkshire and Scotland, but as to the size of each or the total number of fellowships he professed ignorance. I felt there was a tendency on his part of optimistic exaggeration. At one time he referred to a series of meetings held in Liverpool, which several hundred attended, as a revival. I am drawn to the conclusion that these groups are not as significant as their leaders would maintain. They appear to follow the Puritan tradition of small Holiness meetings, and I would venture their future expansion or even existence is uncertain.

The Church at South Chard (Somerset)

The church at South Chard was one of the forerunners of the Charismatic Movement in the United Kingdom. The founders were a Mr Sidney Purse and his wife, who belonged to a Brethren Assembly. Their work began in the village of South Chard in the post war years when they taught a Sunday School class. By 1949 there were forty children attending. About this time both claimed to have received the experience of the Baptism in the Spirit, after which relationships in the Brethren Assembly became tense and they were obliged to. leave.

They began to hold meetings in their home, the Manor House, which became a house church, to the extent that Mr Purse dug a baptistry in the living room. Their aim was to encourage individuals, and later as the work expanded, communities, to return to the New Testament patterns of Christian experience and church life.

In 1952 the site of the church at South Chard was bought. It is situated next to the Manor House. Mr Purse himself played a major part in the building of the church as he was by trade a bricklayer.

The present church building was opened in 1956. The concept of a house church is still maintained as the church stands only forty feet from the house, and the work of the two - house and church - are closely related. Accommodation is readily available for those wishing to visit the church, and many do visit, from individuals to groups from churches and house fellowships. The church is rarely without visitors, both from the U.K. and abroad.

There has been no conscious aim to encourage house churches to begin, but as the church became known, requests for help began to arrive. Frequently the men in the church are asked to help and support small groups who are just starting a house church, or even to give advice where a new beginning is desired and counsel is required on how to start. One of the features of the church is the high proportion of young men who have made themselves available for this kind of itinerant ministry.

When such a request for help has been made and after consultation a house church is formed, further visits are made until the new church is strong enough to proceed. This help is given on an informal friendly basis, without any insistence on translocal authority. Accordingly these house churches will insist that they are completely independent; they resist any suggestion that they "belong" to the church at South Chard.

The men of the church travel extensively to almost every part of the world. There is no sense of exclusivism as they preach and minister in all Christian groups, from the traditional denominations to charismatic groups, Pentecostal and house churches.(3)

This church stands closer to the original Pentecostal tradition than do the Harvestime churches and North fellowships.

The influence of the church at South Chard is considerable, both in cases where house churches have been formed through their encouragement, and in the instances of help and support that they have given to groups from denominational churches. They are undoubtedly a very important force in the growth of the House Church Movement.

These three groups form the main pattern of the House Church Movement. There are still instances of house churches not affiliated in any way with any other group. Since the impact of the Harvestime Churches, particularly after 1975, these independent churches are not so numerous, as many then saw the advantages of belonging to a larger network. But they still exist - in what proportion it would not be easy to ascertain - and it is safe to say that most House Churches in this country fall into one of the three categories mentioned.

These three are very different from each other as will be seen from the examination of organisation and worship, although the lifestyle of each type of fellowship bears much similarity. In considering examples of certain local churches the history of the formation of each one will again indicate similar situations. Most appear to have materialised out of tensions and dissatisfactions in the existing church situation.

The information in this chapter was given exclusively by interviews with the founders of the churches concerned. Therefore it should be stated that although I have attempted to present the material objectively it is basically an account of the formation of their movement seen through their interpretation.

The following six examples have been taken to give an indication of how certain local house churches came into existence. Five of the six arose from a different denominational situation: Baptist, Brethren, Methodist, Anglican, Pentecostal. In four cases small groups of people joined together to find a more relevant Christianity and reality of worship than they already knew. In two cases pastors of churches resigned from what had become intolerable situations, in both cases a schism resulted in the church. The birth of these house churches has not been easy, each has been the product of tension, stress and misunderstanding. The reason is basically that there are those who want change in religious life, and those who view such changes as dangerous innovations.

The Harvestime Group

1. Chester - The Church of the Way (1)

Goos Vedder, the first pastor of the church at Chester, was originally a member of the Dutch Reformed Church. Following a conversion experience he and his parents were baptised by immersion. They were then asked to leave the Dutch Reformed Church, and so they joined a Pentecostal Assembly.

Goos Vedder first met Bryn and Keri Jones when he came to England to train for Christian service at the Bible College of South Wales. After working with a team of evangelists in Holland for three years whose main concern was the supply of Bibles and Christian literature to Communist countries he met and married an English girl and in October 1970 came to this country to live.

Until January 1974 they lived in a Cotswold village and he worked as an evangelist, travelling in this country and making several excursions to Eastern Europe, in particular to Rumania and Czechoslovakia, with Bibles, religious literature and tape and cassette recorders for the Christians there. Then he was invited to become the full time Pastor of Hoole Baptist Church. This was a church which had taken an interest in his activities in Eastern Europe, at which he had been a frequent speaker. So he felt he was moving into a situation where he was known and accepted.

Nevertheless within a year serious difficulties arose. During that year the church members saw their church change from a typical Baptist church to something they felt was alien. There was an influx of young people and younger married couples who supported the Pastor in the pentecostal type of worship which they enjoyed. Looking back Goos Vedder saw the tensions lay in three areas.

1. He was criticised for teaching the doctrine of the Baptism in the Spirit every Sunday. He maintained his teaching was centred on faith and subjects concerned with the Kingdom of God.

2. He was censured for neglecting to visit the elderly in their homes - a
traditional duty for every minister. He admits this was a justified
criticism and says he saw his duty was to give his time to those in the
church who were "born again" and not to spend time visiting those who
had no personal faith.

3. The previous part time Pastor stayed on in the church as an Elder. This
situation lent itself to comparison and criticism.

Matters came to a head at a church members' meeting. The church members
consisted of the long standing members of the church. The newer younger element had not bothered to become members. It was stated at the meeting that
the present situation was not right and a vote of no confidence in the minister
was taken. A majority of two thirds was required before any action could be
taken, and half the members voted against the Pastor, so the situation was
virtually a stalemate.

Goos Vedder asked the local superintendent of the Baptist Union to come
from Manchester to give him some advice. Although he was very understanding
he said there was nothing he could do; without a majority of two thirds the
members could not ask the Pastor to resign. As half the church members supported him together with the regular churchgoers who were not members Goos
Vedder was in a fairly strong position. But the situation was not a happy
one and so he decided to leave.

He contacted Bryn Jones for counsel and then took the following course
of action: He did not give the customary three months notice of leaving, but
took one more service the following Sunday. There he spoke for about three
minutes to explain to the congregation that half of the church members had
no confidence in his ministry, and he felt it was better he should go at
once so that the church could grow in the way they felt the Lord was leading
them. He said if any of those present felt they had a relationship with him
as sheep have to a shepherd they could contact him during the week, to find
out what the Lord had put on their hearts to do next.

During the following week Goos Vedder heard that there was a room in
the shopping complex,known as the Arts Centre, which was available for hire
on Sunday. As people telephoned that week they were told that there would
be a meeting on Sunday morning in the Arts Centre. That first Sunday morning
one hundred people came, but it was obvious that word had travelled around
Chester as to what had happened, and people known to be interested in charismatic worship from all different churches in the area were there. It appeared
that many thought this was to be a Pentecostal "picnic".

From the start Goos Vedder made it clear this was to be a fellowship with
an emphasis on authority and submission to authority. Many then left and
returned to their original churches. Nine from Hoole Baptist Church stayed
with Goos Vedder. Of these, two of the men are now Elders in the church.

In February 1975 Bryn Jones, Keri Jones and Peter Paris came to commis-
sion Goos Vedder as Pastor of the new church. At a mid-week meeting at the
Arts Centre Bryn Jones commissioned him by "setting him before the church"
to acknowledge him as their Pastor. He was then also "set before" the other
shepherds present, Keri Jones and Peter Paris, as a shepherd and a Pastor.

38

Thus acknowledged, the new minister and church began.

The numbers in the church dropped to thirty by September 1975. From that point in time the church began to consolidate. Those who had come for a good time had gone. Those who came knew the type of fellowship it was.

Each year a contingent from the church has attended the summer convention; in 1975 the teaching of Ern Baxter on the understanding of the government of democratic institutions contrasted with the divine appointments in the desired structure of the church. This further developed the teaching on authority which Goos Vedder had already given the church.

In February 1976 Rob Watts was appointed an Elder, whilst continuing his full time secular work. In the summer of 1976 Goos Vedder went with a friend, Andrew Harmsworth, to the Shetland Islands. Andrew Harmsworth, a grandson of the owner of the Harmsworth Press, had met Goos Vedder whilst studying at the Royal Agricultural College, Cirencester, close to the Vedders' home. He was working on Shetland and asked Goos Vedder to come to speak to local Christians. The result was that Goos Vedder, together with Dave Richards of Merryfield House, Witney, is now responsible for two groups in the islands of Papastour and Shetland, one of which was a former hippy colony.

In February 1977 it was recognised that Dave Coles, a science teacher in a local boys' public school, had leadership potential, and accordingly he began to take part and be drawn into the activities of the Elders. After a year he was officially declared an Elder.

In November 1976 steps were taken to acquire a Christian bookshop. After buying an existing Christian bookshop on the outskirts of town more suitable premises were acquired in the centre of town.

In November 1977 Bryn Jones asked Goos Vedder to be responsible for a group of thirty adults in Worthen, near Shrewsbury. In June 1978 a small group in Prestatyn who had attended some meetings in Chester asked Goos Vedder to be Pastor of their group. In September 1978 Bryn Jones again asked him to take a further group of twenty-five adults in Nottingham. So his work developed in other areas, whilst the Elders in Chester carried on the ministry of the home church during his absence. Rob Watts and Dave Coles were both brought into full time ministry.

Early in 1979 the church moved into a new building. For some time it was felt that the Arts Centre was unsuitable - before services could be held on Sunday litter and beer cans had to be swept away. It was also very difficult to hire during the week, and as church members grew to over a hundred it was no longer practicable to meet in a home.

In December 1977 Dave Coles, Rob Watts and Goos Vedder were all at a leaders' conference when news came that the Arts Centre had burnt down. Temporarily they met in the YMCA, then in January 1978 they considered buying a disused church. That needed too much renovation, but then a former Congregational church was put up for sale. For some years this had been used by the local College of Education, but the college had now completed a new building programme and the owners wanted to sell.

The Elders of the church were somewhat surprised to learn that the Congregational Church stated through their Estate Agent that they wanted the church to be sold as a commercial warehouse. They refused Goos Vedder's offer, but at the subsequent auction sale the church, being one of three interested parties, bought the building for £17,500. The one hundred members of the church gave £3,000, loaned £3,000 free of interest, and the rest was obtained on loan from the bank.

The new church is situated on one of the main thoroughfares of the city. Permission has been obtained for the outbuildings to be used for religious education and community work. The name of the church at Chester will be changed, to identify with the new building. As that was always known as Northgate Congregational Church, the Church of the Way has now become simply Northgate Church, a new name as the church enters a new phase in its history. Early in 1981 Goos Vedder moved to Bradford to work on the apostolic team there.

The story of this church has centred around the personality of Goos Vedder. This was his first appointment as Pastor and he had had no previous experience of a pastoral ministry. From the early days of his appointment there was tension and dissatisfaction felt by longstanding members of the church, both in the way he conducted services and in his attitudes to older members of the church. Goos Vedder admits his concern lay with those in line with his views who were as he says "going on with the Lord", and not with the elderly and infirm who had been Baptists all their lives. It is easy to understand the disquiet felt by some, but here was a dichotomy concerning the question of what constituted a membership of the church: Life-long attendance or a testimony of personal conversion, Baptism in the Spirit, and a desire to submit to the pastor's authority.

For many years Goos Vedder had been a close friend of Bryn and Keri Jones, and as such holds the same concept of a church structured on authority and submission. He attempted to impose that structure on an existing church and quite naturally many members refused to accept his teaching. In observing this particular church it is obvious that it is run on authoritarian lines amounting at times to severity. There are no half measures, the members either submit to the Elders or leave, and very many have left. No individual decision may be taken without prior consultation with the Elders - to rebel against them is to rebel against God.

2. The Solihull Christian Fellowship(2)

This church began when a group of people realised they wanted a deeper, more satisfying Christian fellowship than was at that time available to them.

The story began in the Solihull Gospel Hall. Brian and Pat Clarke(3) had moved to Solihull from Hertfordshire in February 1969. Previously they had attended a house church in Richmond, Surrey, and they looked for a similar fellowship in Solihull. Brian had originally been a member of the Salvation Army, but Pat had always known the background of the house church. Her parents had left China during the 1920s and settled in Malaya. They had come out of the Methodist Church and begun a house church, which had progressed and expanded until a church building had been built. In the early years they were encouraged by the visits of Watchman Nee who was an old friend of Pat's father.

In Solihull neither felt attracted to the denominations and eventually they attended the Brethren Assembly at the Solihull Gospel Hall. There they met and formed a firm friendship with Stephen and Jeanne Wood.

Stephen Wood had been a lifelong member of the Brethren Movement, but for some time he and his wife had felt that the worship in the Assembly was too stereotyped and steeped in tradition to be open to the working of the Spirit of God.

They began to have informal Bible studies with another couple who were new members of the Assembly. This study group grew until they were about ten in number. They then decided to leave the Brethren and attend Acocks Green Baptist Church; there they met others who were to help found the nucleus of the present fellowship. Alan and Heather Cameron had moved to the area from Walton-on-Thames. Joy Kinnersley returned to Solihull after a period of teaching in Stafford. The group found that they had a lot in common with the minister Bill Rogers who was very interested in the Charismatic Movement.

Bill Rogers became very concerned that the church in Acocks Green, although it attracted a good membership, did not serve the neighbourhood; the congregation came from other areas. He was particularly concerned that a nucleus of people in his church came from Solihull because they had no-where compatible where they could worship in their own town.

In March 1971 they turned the Bible study into a prayer meeting; Brian and Pat Clarke joined them and Bill Rogers gave three months notice of leaving to the Baptist Church. Together the small fellowship provided a house for him where on the first Sunday in September they held the first meeting. The first steps had been taken to begin a new church in Solihull.

After only six months Bill Rogers left the group. It was realised that he wanted to have the role of minister, whereas the others felt they needed some new structure, albeit as yet undefined. Rogers left and became the minister of the Memorial Church at Lapworth, a village outside Warwick.

The meetings were continued at Brian and Pat Clarke's home for the next two years. They were joined by Jonathan and Sylvia Wallis (the son of Arthur Wallis, a well known speaker and writer). They too were formerly of the Brethren Movement. In these early days about twenty-four people attended the meetings.

In January 1972 Stephen Wood went to a weekend conference at the Richmond Fellowship. This was to be the turning point in the life of the church, for there he met Hugh Thompson and heard him preach. He felt very attracted to this type of teaching, which emphasises the government and authority of God and speaks of how God is working in his Church today by calling people together. In May 1972 he began a correspondence with Hugh Thompson which led to the latter subsequently visiting the fellowship.

Since the time they had left the Baptist Church they had been encouraged by visits from Arthur Wallis,and gradually the character of the meetings had changed to that of a Pentecostal type of worship. Stephen Wood recalls that during the eighteen months since he had left the Brethren Assembly he was gradually changing and softening in his attitude towards Pentecostalism.

In the new year of 1972 Stephen Wood had an experience of the Baptism in the Spirit; shortly afterwards Alan and Heather Cameron entered into the same experience. The Clarkes and Jonathan and Sylvia Wallis were already involved in Charismatic Renewal, and so by March 1972 all the members of the fellowship had entered into this particular experience. Throughout this fellowship has been characterised by a desire for a more relevant realistic way of worship; they were determined to break with stereotyped tradition.

The group were beginning to feel they should have a leader. When Hugh Thompson visited early in 1974 he asked around the group whom they would like to see as leader. At the time this was unknown to Stephen Wood, who for some time had felt a deep concern for the people in the fellowship - he describes this feeling as that "he believed he had a shepherding heart". Most of the fellowship mentioned Stephen's name to Hugh Thompson as a possible Elder. The following Sunday the fellowship fasted and prayed and felt they had a promise from God when there was a word of prophecy that God would establish leadership in the group. The next occasion Hugh Thompson visited he was told of this word of prophecy, the question of leadership was discussed and it was decided that Stephen Wood had indicated that he had the qualities of a shepherd. Soon after, at a special service on a Sunday evening, Arthur Wallis, Hugh Thompson and the fellowship considered the subject of shepherding. Arthur Wallis and Hugh Thompson prayed for Stephen and Jeanne and laid hands on them. There were words of prophecy from Hugh Thompson concerning Stephen's role as Elder and from Arthur Wallis concerning Jeanne's role as his wife.

Stephen was the sole Elder of the fellowship for twelve months. Then Allan Cameron was appointed Elder by Hugh Thompson and David Tomlinson. Allan Cameron and his family subsequently moved to Walsall in order to establish a church there. Eighteen months later Brian Pullinger was appointed Elder by David Tomlinson and Arthur Wallis. Brian Pullinger was an old school friend of Stephen Wood, he and his wife Jenny had joined the group from Bentley Heath, Brethren Assembly.

When Hugh Thompson moved from Bristol to Middlesbrough, David Tomlinson who was at Ripon eventually joined him. A change in the Apostleship of the Solihull church then occurred. At first it was decided that together the two would act as Apostles to the churches in their care. This did not work out; basically the two men fulfil very different ministries. Hugh Thompson is seen to be a teacher and a prophet and David Tomlinson is more a builder of churches. Accordingly David Tomlinson came once with Hugh Thompson to Solihull and then the sole care of the church was passed on to him. He now visits on a regular basis, usually every eight weeks. There are several churches in the area to which he has the authority of an Apostle; he usually spends two nights at Solihull. In the meantime Hugh Thompson is now involved in the Harvestime publishing work.

For three years from 1973 to 1976 the fellowship occupied the Penthouse Suite in the Civic Hall. This proved to be very comfortable, but when the children's work grew so that separate rooms were needed the fellowship moved to its present location in a Secondary School. This move was facilitated by a member of the fellowship who is on the staff of the school.

The difficult opening phases in the life of this church are over; it has now taken its place as one of the respected Christian churches in the area. By the genuine concern for cooperation with other Christian groups they now enjoy a good working relationship with many other churches. There is a more relaxed atmosphere than was felt in the previous example of the church at Chester. These are a group of people who are anxious to maintain harmony both within their own group and with other Christian churches. The emphasis on authority is implicit rather than explicit, but nevertheless it is there. Here it is expressed in the exhortation to "listen to what God is saying", which presumably is what God is saying to the Elders.

This church only admits those who live in the area as committed members, and discourages regular attendance from those who travel from other districts, unless they are preparing to start up a new church in their own town. Should any from other towns show interest in the Solihull Fellowship it is suggested they move into the town, and continual pressure is brought to bear with this aim in view. Practical considerations such as professional commitments must take second place to what is termed "living in the body", i.e. near the Christians in the church. So in essence the same authoritarian care is there, albeit expressed in a very friendly manner.

3. The Church at Merryfield House, Witney(4)

In 1971 a group of young people in the Methodist Church at Witney attended a youth weekend. During the meetings twelve of the group, including four youth leaders, professed a conversion experience, somewhat to the latter's embarrassment. They realised they had spent years working in the Methodist organisations but that being a Christian meant more than performing good works. The leaders were two married couples, Dave and Christine Richards and Geoff and Mary Norridge. Of the twelve who professed conversion, eight are now in the Church at Merryfield House.

The Methodist Church at Witney did not have an evangelical ministry. The four leaders began to meet together, they prayed and read the Bible, but after a year they felt discouraged, feeling it was not leading them anywhere and that they needed to find reality.

Then an Anglican minister, Howard Cole, came to preach at the Methodist church one Sunday. He was the vicar of the Anglican church in the village of Cogges near Witney(5) and was associated with the Fountain Trust. After the service the four made arrangements to visit Cole at his home that evening. That afternoon as they prayed together the two men were baptised in the Spirit, their wives entered into the experience a few days later.

Subsequently Howard Cole called a group together who were interested in the Charismatic Movement. He seems to have been encouraged by contact with the four; previously, like many of the early charismatics, he had received much criticism and opposition which made him nervous and reticent to begin any charismatic meetings. Now however he hoped to be able to work and have fellowship with the four. However, they only went twice to his meetings - they felt he was moving too slowly. So they began to hold meetings in the

Norridge's bungalow at Minster Lovell, a village outside Witney. People from around the area began to come, including the young people from the Methodist church, until about fifty were present.

At the same time the two couples, with two single girls, began to meet to pray for a place in the centre of Witney where they could have a Christian family centre. Dave and Christine had from the beginning been involved in an exorcism and counselling ministry. For two years they met every day to pray. They believe God spoke to them through a word of prophecy that they would have a place from which they could centre their activities.

Several times they visited the church at South Chard. On one occasion they went as families with their children, and on another they took the young people of the church to Devon on holiday and stayed near enough to attend the service. They were impressed. Men from Chard visited their meetings and in the early days helped and encouraged them a great deal.

At that time Merryfield House came into the picture. The two single girls had rented it for use as a Christian guesthouse, then the owner, a David Smith, sold it to a developer. The house was built in 1927 but in the style of an old Oxford farmhouse.

In July 1973 the Minister of the Environment put a preservation order on the house, four days before it was due to be demolished. The two married couples saw this as an answer to the two years of prayer and both sold their homes in order to buy it. The purchase price was £28,000. After the central heating was installed they still owed £12,000. People from all parts of the country, many of whom they did not know, had contacted them to give them donations towards a purchase price. They attempted to obtain a mortgage for the remaining twelve thousand pounds and here met difficulties. Eighteen building societies refused, the reason being that they distrusted the situation of two families living together. The local Council offered a substantial mortgage if the couples stated the house would be divided into separate accommodation. As this was not true they refused. Their solicitor wrote a disclaimer on the situation. Then a woman whom they did not know telephoned to say she had heard about their situation and wanted to help. She asked what their need was and offered to provide £12,000 as a private mortgage. So they acquired the house. The two single girls who had run the house as a Christian guesthouse had documents which allowed it to be used for religious teaching, so the way was clear for their work to begin. What form it would take they did not know, but subsequent events were moulded by the circumstances which arose in the Methodist church.

All four were still employed in secular work: Dave and Christine were teaching, Dave being deputy head of a large junior school; Geoff also was a teacher and Mary a physiotherapist.

In September 1973 they moved into the house. In the meantime the situation in the Methodist church was becoming increasingly awkward. That year Goos Vedder, who was living in Clanfield, began Saturday seminars. Various charismatic speakers came and hundreds converged on the small village, many travelling long distances. Many people went to Clanfield from Witney.

The garden at Merryfield House contained a swimming pool. Slowly the four began to see the importance of water baptism and they began to hold baptism services in the swimming pool. They were careful always to ensure permission was asked of the minister of the individuals concerned if the enquirer was an adult, and of the parents if a juvenile. In every case the ministers gave consent. Some of the parents refused and their wishes were always respected.

The situation came to a climax in the local Methodist church when Goos Vedder was invited to speak at a youth meeting after the Sunday evening service. All the Methodist ministers from the area were present, including their own minister. Goos Vedder spoke on various texts from the Book of Revelation - this sermon caused a hostile reaction, largely because of the length; he spoke for over two hours.

The immediate result was felt when most of the young people who had booked for a weekend conference, arranged by the four youth leaders, decided not to attend. Victor Gledhill from Basingstoke(6), an ex-missionary from Nepal, had been invited as speaker, so the four took the remaining group which met in their home.

After that time none of the four were allowed to organise any youth activities in the Methodist church. Someone older was detailed to oversee any arrangements. Then the organisation of the church was completely restructured with new committees for every organisation and activity. During the elections the four youth leaders were not re-elected to any office. They felt totally rejected.

In September 1974 the minister asked the two men, Geoff and Dave, to meet him. He asked two questions. Firstly, "How do you see your movement fitting into this church in particular and the Methodist Church as a whole?" and secondly, "How can we help you, and you help us?" They were asked to go away and consider these two aspects.

They returned to talk to the minister about two weeks later. They admitted they had been enthusiastic and thereby probably offended. The minister expressed the opinion that they were wrong to be practising baptisms in their garden. Both Geoff and Dave felt hurt and puzzled because they had asked permission in each case for a member of his church to be baptised and this had always been given; moreover, the minister had repeatedly been invited to the baptism services.

He asked them to explain what they understood by baptism, and why they felt they had the authority to baptise and why they baptised adults. They explained they saw baptism as a mark of discipleship and therefore a necessary step in the life of the adult believer. The disciples of Jesus baptised and they were not ordained, therefore they felt they were able to follow that example.

The minister replied that to remain Methodists and believe what they did was hypocritical. They asked if he was telling them to leave the church. He said he would never throw them out. The minister was, they felt, a man of compromise; he did not enjoy such a confrontation. They then offered to resign their membership of the church. The minister seemed relieved and expressed the opinion that it was a good solution.

The two wives were unhappy at the thought of leaving their friends - they all felt rejected. The minister seemed unhappy at the outcome. But from that time the work of the church at Merryfield House began to grow.

Dave Richards saw that a crisis point in his life was the time of his baptism in water. This caused a revolution in his thinking - he began to grow in his desire to care for people.

The first thing the four did when they left the Methodist church was to contact Vic Gledhill at Basingstoke to ask for help. They began to meet on Sundays deliberately at the same time as the church services so that they would not influence church members by enabling them to attend both services. They impressed upon each one who came that they should not leave the denom- inational church just because they themselves had left, but only as each received a clear word from God. Fifty people were then attending their mid-week meeting; within six months thirty, claiming direction from God, had joined them on Sundays. This direction could come in several ways - through reading a particular passage in the Bible which seemed to indicate they should join the fellowship, through a word of prophecy, or simply through a growing conviction. This direction must also be confirmed through the leaders, who pay particular attention to the text in Acts 2:47 which says that the Lord adds to the church, the leaders are not the active force. They do however expect people to worship only in one place, so that those who come on Sundays are expected to commit themselves; this also safeguards other ministers in the town, so that their church members are not taking Sundays off to visit a more exciting fellowship.

When Christine and Goos Vedder moved from Clanfield to Chester in December 1974, Dave Richards took over the organisation of the Saturday seminars. They moved the venue from Clanfield to Merryfield House. During 1975 it was felt that the seminars had served their purpose to give a vision of what the church could be. They had provided a foundational ministry, but now the time had come to concentrate on the local area, rather than continue to attract people from wide distances.

Vic Gledhill and Barney Coombs(7) from the Basingstoke church came to "set in" Dave and Geoff as Elders. They laid hands on them and prophesied. At that time there were forty committed church members.

At Easter 1976 Dave Richards gave up his teaching career to become a full time pastor and in August of that year Geoff followed suit.

In May 1976 Dave went on his first trip to the Shetlands with Goos Vedder, then during September and October Geoff and Dave spent six weeks in Nepal visiting the communities where Vic Gledhill had worked. They took twenty-six meetings in ten days, then went on to Katmandu where they found a fellowship of one thousand Christians.

On 2st January 1978 John Wastie, a painter and decorator, joined them as an Elder, so at the present time they have three full time Elders who are concerned with shepherding the members, and a fourth Elder still in secular employment,who has a prophetic ministry.

The Sunday meetings are now held in a local school as the house will no longer comfortably accommodate all 168 members.

Other fellowships have sprung up, encouraged by the support of those at
Merryfield House. These are at Cote, Kidlington, Cirencester and Nottingham.
In April 1979 after discussion it was decided that Dave Richards should be
released for itinerant work amongst these fellowships and any others that
should emerge.

After some years of tension the church at Merryfield House is now established and thriving. The Elders, however, are anxious to emphasise that they
see this not as a result of their efforts but as God working in that area;
they stress repeatedly they are not building an organisation but allowing the
Spirit of God to work.

An honest straightforward account was given of the difficulties experienced in the Methodist church leading up to the formation of the church at
Merryfield House. They admit they caused offence through over enthusiasm,
but it appears the differences were theological more than a clash of personalities. Previously all four were in positions of trust in the Methodist
church. Following certain personal spiritual experiences which led to a
change of emphasis on the part of the two couples, relationships deteriorated
between themselves and the minister who was unwilling to encourage a departure from the Methodist traditions and practice. No doubt a schism was inevitable as the four were gathering a counter group of those interested in
their particular style of worship.

The day to day life of this church and the growing numbers indicate
a very happy community. As a discipling concept is practised on a one to
one basis there is not the same stress placed on the authority of the Elders
as in the previous churches examined. Each new individual or family is
placed under the "covering" of another member and will in turn to be called
upon to disciple the next person joining the church. Thus relationships are
as a chain linking the community together.

Schism in a church is always unfortunate, but can it sometimes be the
best solution for a dichotomous situation? This church has brought a new way
of worship and a new way of life to a rural part of England which has not seen
such an innovation in religion since John Wesley preached to a repentant village community in the aftermath of a dramatic storm in July 1783.

The North Fellowships

1. The Russell House Fellowship, Leamington Spa (8)

Dave Orange was an agricultural worker from an evangelical Anglican background. In 1971 he married Penny Shilling, when he was twenty-one and she
eighteen years of age. Shortly after their marriage Dave lost his job and
their tied cottage, because he refused to work on Sundays. On reflection now
he feels this was a display of youthful arrogance. However, they went to
live for some months at the home of the curate of St Mary's Church, Leamington
Spa.

The curate had for some time been planning to open a coffee bar in the town to operate as a business venture during the day, and a form of evangelistic outreach in the evenings. His vicar supported him in this, and eventually premises were purchased and "The Fisherman" was opened as an ecumenical concern supported in theory by the churches in the town; in practice it was run by two salaried staff and a team of volunteers from St Mary's Church, helped occasionally by a few from the Methodist church.

In February 1973 Penny was appointed the manageress, Dave obtained work on a building site, and they lived in the flat above the coffee bar. They had for some time been prominent members of the church youth group and were very popular with younger members - a fact which was to prove significant later.

In the summer of 1973 the church, with the help of the local authority, purchased an old warehouse in a poor quarter of the town and opened a youth centre there. Dave Orange voluntarily supervised all the activities.

From that time various events happened in the life of the church fellowship which Dave and Penny found increasingly hurtful.

At the coffee bar there were difficulties in the evenings made by gangs of youths. Several times the Police were called to deal with situations that were beyond control. Finally the vicar called together those interested in the work of The Fisherman. It was decided the coffee bar should open for business only during the daytime. Penny and Dave felt their opinions as those most closely concerned with The Fisherman should have been considered.

Then the vicar divided his congregation into seven fellowships concerned with different aspects of church life - music, the youth centre, the care of the elderly; individuals could choose which fellowship to attend unless they were actually involved in a certain area of work. So it was that Dave who ran the youth centre found that he and Penny, who was in the singing group, were to attend different groups. As all their spare time was used in church work they felt this was an unnecessary separation.

Of that time Dave speaks of feeling a great spiritual hunger coupled with a longing to evangelise. St Mary's Church was situated in a poor district, people came to the church because it was known to be "friendly". Frequently they had problems - of drugs, marital problems, criminal offences. He felt the church was not answering their needs.

At Easter 1973 he and Penny went to a charismatic conference at Haldon Court, Exmouth. It was led by men who are now Elders in the Harvestime Churches. They both felt that there was more to Christianity than what they heard in church, and they were determined to find out what it was.

In the area of the church fellowship meetings, that concerned with the youth centre - of which Dave was the leader - saw a change in the content of the meeting. More emphasis was placed on worship of a charismatic nature. Others began to leave their groups and move into that one. Eventually the vicar decided to change the leadership.

Each fellowship took a turn at leading the Sunday evening service once

a month. When it was the turn of the youth centre fellowship Dave spoke at
the close on the theme that a Christian is not under law but under grace -
"It is not what you can do for Christ, but what he can do for you". After
the service the vicar took Dave aside to express his concern at the emphasis
of his talk.

In the summer of 1974 a group of young people from the church went on an
exchange visit to New York and Florida. Dave and Penny Orange were among the
group. During a visit to the Teen Challenge Centre for drug addicts of the
evangelist David Wilkerson, Dave Orange claims he had a spiritual experience
when he remained behind in the chapel - in tears as he realised the love and
compassion of God for these addicts.

Back in England the vicar had begun to emphasise the importance of
church members accepting his authority and submitting to him. Many hitherto
faithful members of the church left at that point. When he preached the
vicar emphasised the necessity of service and the importance of good works
in the life of the Christian. There was obviously a growing dichotomy between the vicar and Dave Orange, each emphasising one facet of Christian experience. One Sunday Dave Orange felt so frustrated at what was being said
that he flung his Bible onto the pew and left the church. Afterwards he and
Penny talked to the vicar and they agreed to differ.

That summer of 1974 had also brought a new and important influence into
their lives. In August they visited a farm at Ab Lench near Evesham where a
Pentecostal summer camp is held every year. On the way home after an evening
meeting their car broke down. They telephoned the farm and the speaker,
Derek Gitsham, who was just leaving for his home in Worcester, came out to
help. He drove them home to Leamington and because it was late stayed the
night. A few weeks later they visited his house church at Worcester - after
that there were no further contacts for some time.

Penny and Dave began to realise that they could no longer stay in the
Anglican Church. They realised they could not submit to the vicar's authority
if they did not agree to what he said and did.

Accordingly after the evening service one Sunday evening in October they
approached the curate with whom they had been friends for years and told him
they had decided to leave the church. The curate immediately asked the vicar
to join them and a heated discussion developed. The vicar accused them of
attending Pentecostal meetings in the area; as the couple had visited none of
those mentioned they were hurt, because they felt they had been loyal to the
church and were now acting sincerely according to their conscience.

Next day the vicar and his wife and the curate and his wife sent bouquets
of flowers, but Penny and Dave thought that a pointless gesture. They sent
letters of resignation to the vicar and also to the Parochial Church Council
as they were both members.

The immediate result of this action was that a group of young people
also declared they had left the church, and those who were on the electoral
roll wrote letters to the P.C.C. announcing the fact. Faced with this group
who looked to him for leadership Dave began to hold meetings in their flat
above The Fisherman. They never seriously considered joining another church.

When the vicar realised what was happening they were forbidden to hold
meetings on the premises of The Fisherman, and Dave was told that he must
not attempt to go to the Youth Centre again as his influence amongst the
young people was undesirable.

For a time they continued to hold their meetings in the house of two
sisters who belonged to their group, and then they moved to the home of a West
Indian family whose daughters were members. By that time the tenancy of their
flat was drawing to a close. Penny was expecting a baby and she would no
longer be able to continue as manageress of The Fisherman, so they had to
find alternative accommodation.

On 1st May 1975 when their son, Daniel, was seven days old they left
The Fisherman and went to live with Penny's parents for six weeks. Then a
member of St Mary's congregation who had moved to Canada offered them his
house in return for payment of his mortgage instalments. They moved into
the three bedroomed detached house which became the focal point of their work.

Dave sees an important stage in the development of their fellowship came
after they had left the church. People no longer called to see him, he had
much more free time and used it to be alone and to pray.

Then two women from the local Brethren Assembly attended one of Mr
G.W. North's conferences at Rora House, Exeter. On the way home their car
broke down. They telephoned home for help but everyone was out, so they
phoned the Oranges. Dave went down to Bristol and towed them home. On the
way home one of the women started to play some taped messages of the conference. Dave was so impressed that he borrowed the set - they were a set of
sermons given by Mr North.

Dave then began seriously to consider the fellowship. He felt they lay
between the evangelicals on the one side and the charismatics on the other -
he realised he needed advice. He himself was young, had received no formal
Bible School training, and he could visualise their little group stagnating.
He thought of two people to whom he could go for advice. One was David
Mansell (a leader in the Harvestime Churches he had met at Exmouth); the
other was Derek Gitsham, whom he had met the previous summer. He decided,
because Derek Gitsham lived much nearer (at Worcester), that he would go to
him.

He recalls feeling nervous. He remembers that the interview took place
in his host's bedroom, because he was tired and taking a rest. Dave remembers
pacing up and down the bedroom, talking of his anxieties for the fellowship,
his host rarely speaking. The outcome of that meeting was a formation of a
close alliance between the Oranges and Derek Gitsham. The group from
Leamington attended Bible Studies at Worcester.

At home Dave Orange began reading John Wesley's sermons. He began to
introduce the idea in this preaching that a Christian could live without sin.
Immediately this brought charges of heresy from Christians in the town. The
vicar of their former church came to express his concern in person. At that
meeting Dave offered to return to his former work at the Youth Centre. He
asked if he could meet with the Parochial Church Council to ask their permission. It was a skeleton P.C.C. who met, not the full council; they refused

his offer. Other charismatic leaders in the town also met with them at that time; the Oranges were told they should join a church and not attempt to run their own fellowship. Dave and Penny realised that apart from the few who met with them they could expect little support from the Christians in Leamington.

Derek Gitsham began to come to Leamington on a regular if intermittent basis. He would take a series of talks for about six weeks, then later return for another series.

Once again the Oranges had to move. The owners of their house decided to settle in Canada and to sell their house in England. The Oranges could not afford to buy it so it was sold to a member of St Mary's congregation. He insisted on immediate possession, so just after their second child was born Penny and Dave again found themselves living with Penny's parents.

At this stage they were determined to own their own home. Dave was then working for a Christian builder; his salary was not enough for him to be accepted by a building society as a prospective borrower, so they approached the local Council who were willing to consider applications for mortgages from people rejected by building societies. They submitted an application for a large house in the southern part of the town, but an Indian offered cash. Derek Gitsham then offered to mortgage his house to provide a lump sum to buy a house.

Then they saw a house - next to the canal and surrounded by workshops, garages, derelict houses and a bakery - priced at only £6,000. But the Council said there was a Clearance Order on the area, and they gave up. A little later Penny met the owner of the house who asked why they had changed their minds. When told about the Clearance Order she contacted the local M.P., Dudley Smith, who in turn contacted the local Council. Apparently the Clearance Order had been rescinded, but the information had not filtered through to all the departments concerned.

In December 1976 the Oranges bought the house, retaining the name, Russell House. In May 1978 the Post Office, who owned the adjoining house, contacted them to say they wished to demolish it to lay underground pipes to the new Telephone Exchange. As the two houses were originally constructed as one, and the division into two had been done unevenly, the Oranges benefited by several extra rooms from the demolition.

Their aim was to have a family home, where people in need can stay. They have helped several young people who were on probation, or ex-convicts; they work in cooperation with the social services.

In the Spring of 1977 Dave Orange began to work on his own as a builder and for a year was self employed. Then in June 1978 he decided the demands of the fellowship were such that he would give up secular employment and spend his time in a ministerial capacity.

Dave Orange states he has never tried to build a fellowship - the fellowship has happened, just as people have come to them in need of help because God is working in the lives of people.

The emergence of this house church can be seen as part of the interesting history of St Mary's Leamington Spa, from which all the founder members came. St Mary's has produced some different manifestations of Christian activity. During the incumbency of the previous vicar, the Revd Pat Ashe, Project Vietnam Orphans was established in the work of caring for Vietnamese children and arranging adoptions by English families. The next incumbent began in a burst of popularity, permission from the Bishop of Coventry was obtained to dispense with the Prayer Book liturgy, and the church began an outreach work amongst the poorer districts of the town. The new vicar helped many with personal problems, some in prison, some with marital difficulties. Such people have retained strong feelings of loyalty to him.

At one time Dave and Penny Orange were among his most enthusiastic helpers. Gradually, through misunderstanding, their role changed to one of challenge to the Vicar's authority. Dave and his wife believed sincerely they had gained new insights and interpretation of the Scriptures. Naturally, the Vicar had to attempt to preserve what he saw, equally sincerely, as unity and order in his congregation. The resulting misunderstanding led to the schism. Afterwards, Dave and his wife did not consider joining one of the other churches. They had been so emotionally involved with St Mary's Church that they considered the disillusionment they felt with that church to extend to all organised forms of Christianity. So they decided to begin their own meetings.

This decision earned them the condemnation of most Christians in the town, which is the reason why mainly young people have joined their fellowship. Following their involvement with Derek Gitsham of Worcester further criticism ensued. Derek Gitsham is well known as an adherent of Mr G.W. North whose teaching is viewed with caution by the Evangelicals and Charismatics in the town. Charges of heresy have been frequent and the fellowship is shunned by respectable churchgoers.

2. The Wake Green Road Fellowship, Moseley, Birmingham (9)

The house church in Wake Green Road, Moseley, is the home of Ron and Margaret Bailey. Originally Anglicans, they were involved in the early days of the Charismatic Movement, being active members of the Church, and as such in 1966 entered Birmingham Bible Institute with the aim of training for missionary work. At that time their first child was two weeks old.

During their time at Bible College they decided to sever their contacts with the Anglican Church. Their doubts increased, particularly in the areas of the validity of infant baptism and the organisational structure of the Church, especially the Scriptural authority for the role of Bishop.

During 1968-69, Ron Bailey's final year at Birmingham Bible Institute, he undertook pastoral duties at an independent church which had written to the college asking for someone to come and preach and take services as they had no minister. When his training was finished the Baileys moved to Billesley, where Ron became the Pastor of the church, the Full Gospel Tabernacle, Yardley Wood Road, which was of the Elim tradition.

They found after a time that there had been a long history of quarrels in the church. The previous Pastor, a man of Calvinistic leanings, was asked to leave. There seems to have been tension between the older members of the church and the young people. Ron Bailey maintains that the older people gave assent to Pentecostal teaching but objected when the young people practised Pentecostal worship.

The church was managed by a group of Elders who formed a managing committee. Ron Bailey comments they were excellent businessmen but they had little spiritual stature or authority. This committee objected to certain developments in the services which their new Pastor encouraged. They felt the services were becoming too lively; they approved of singing choruses, but did not agree with enthusiastic clapping. Criticisms were expressed openly in church meetings.

In the late summer of 1971 one Sunday night Ron Bailey told the managing committee he wished to resign, as every aspect of church activity seemed to end in controversy. On the Monday evening the Elders held their regular meeting, on the Tuesday evening Ron Bailey was told not to take the usual Tuesday Bible Study, although he had said he would carry on his duties until a replacement had been found.

At the Bible Study one of the Elders told church members the Pastor had resigned, but that now was the time for them to show loyalty to the church. During the next few days about forty people telephoned the Baileys to ask what would now happen. These forty immediately also left, and so with this schism as a nucleus the house church was formed late in 1971.

The first meeting was held at the Bailey's home on the Sunday evening at 7 p.m. The hour was chosen particularly to enable people to attend the church service. Ron Bailey was surprised to see as many as forty people present. At that first meeting there was a word of prophecy which said God would guide, lead, teach, care for and feed his people, there was mention of the parable of a mother in labour and the exhortation to pay attention to what God was doing - now and what He would do in the future. This was regarded as a direct message from God.

They continued to meet going from house to house without a regular meeting place - at first on Sunday evening, then also one night in the week. Interested visitors were advised to continue going to the church unless absolutely convinced their place was with the house group.

During the next two years numbers grew and then the problem of leadership arose. Ron Bailey was convinced that the Christian Brethren idea of a group of men assuming leadership was right, but formerly he had been the sole Pastor of these people, and they looked to him to continue in that role. For a time he refused to take any part in leadership and insisted that others began to lead. Out of these others one strong character emerged, a much younger man who naturally gravitated to the position of leader. This gave rise to some conflict within the group, as most saw Ron Bailey as the Pastor and felt that he should take a more definite role.

In 1973 the meetings assumed a more settled character when six out of eight flats in a house, 82 Edgbaston Road, Birmingham, were leased by members

53

of the fellowship. From that time all meetings were held at that home.

In 1974 Derek Harrison, the leader of a house church in Wentworth Road, Harborne, Birmingham, invited Ron Bailey and Stephen Wood (of the Solihull Christian Fellowship) to a conference run by Bryn Jones in Birmingham. Barney Coombs of Basingstoke was one of the speakers.

Shortly after that another conference was held at 82, Edgbaston Road, to which the leaders from a house church at Leicester also came. Bryn Jones and Michael Stevens were the speakers.

At that time Ron Bailey felt he needed advice about the problem of leadership in his fellowship. He had long discussions with Bryn Jones who advised him to take authority over his fellowship. He added that Ron also needed to enter into a relationship with other leaders, so that he would have authority over his own people and in turn have the authority of other leaders over him. Bryn Jones offered to have that relationship with him; Ron was at that time attracted to that idea.

Before taking such a step Ron Bailey felt he must discuss with Bryn his own convictions on the spiritual issues surrounding the "new birth". He was invited to Bradford, but when he arrived he found not only Bryn waiting for him but his brother Keri, and Gwyn Daniel and David Tomlinson. The latter had originally been with Mr North in Liverpool and had been sent by him to pastor a church in Ripon, and thence had eventually joined Bryn Jones and his colleagues. His brother Frank however has remained with Mr North. For some time that day Ron Bailey spoke to the group. They listened, they were sympathetic, and they questioned him persistently. When Ron Bailey left, he felt a rift had taken place. He continued to attend Bryn's meetings for leaders at Leicester but he began to feel cautious.

Still feeling isolated, Ron heard through a church member of Norman Meaton in Liverpool. He went to see him to ask his advice on the leadership of his church. Norman Meaton impressed upon him the importance of assuming the leadership of the group, saying that leadership brought responsibilities from which one cannot run away. Ron realised he disliked responsibility, and that he had caused his church to come into being. He became more willing to be the pastor. The young man of strong character was willing to accept this and so for the time being the problem of leadership was solved.

The problem of their wider connections as a church went on. At a conference centre called "The Gaynes" in Bromyard there was a meeting of Elders in 1974 at which Mr. G.W. North was the speaker. Among those present were David Tomlinson, Peter Paris, Bryn Jones, and at that point Ron Bailey felt that one of two alternatives could have happened. There could have emerged one type of house church - in complete harmony - or two distinct chains of fellowships. The second alternative occurred.

The Leicester meetings for Elders continued with a definite emphasis in Bryn's teaching of a declaration of what the Lord was saying to the churches - it seemed there was a different message each year. Ron Bailey had some reservations on this interpretation. A group of house church leaders would attend the Leicester meetings together: himself, Derek Harrison, Martin Williams (Mr North's son-in-law) and Stephen Wood.

In the open discussions which followed the preaching it became an open confrontation between Bryn Jones and the three from Birmingham. The differences between those who followed Mr North's line of thought and those who followed Bryn Jones' concept of church structure were becoming very apparent. Finally Bryn Jones stated that they had had the opportunity to enter into the structure of the fellowships - if they did not now decide to come into relationship with other leaders God would move around them. Only Stephen Wood remained with the Bryn Jones group. The other three felt the relationship had finished, and presently they began a monthly weekend for their fellowships at the same time as the Leicester meetings for Elders, and so the contact with Bryn Jones stopped.

The Baileys had bought a semi-detached house in Kings Heath, early in 1975. This was sold in order to provide the deposit for the house in Wake Green Road. The church now pays the mortgage instalments, but the house is legally in Ron Bailey's name. He has made a will leaving it to his co-leader so that in the event of his death it will pass to this leader to be used for the benefit of the church.

Early in 1976 the question of leadership again became crucial. There were by this time four men acting as Elders and four as Deacons. However, the church was not thriving as it should, and Ron Bailey became convinced that not all four were fulfilling the role of Elder. There was a real need to go back and dismantle the eldership. He contacted Norman Meaton to ask if he would be available for consultation and to support them in prayer.

During the next twelve months they came to a point where all eight men were prepared to relinquish their positions. They brought this issue to the church in a general meeting, faced the situation honestly, and stated that the present leadership was wrong and asked the church to pray. All eight then resigned.

It was the general opinion that there was a need for leadership. They waited another three months. Someone obviously had to organise events - so during this time Ron Bailey as the only trained Pastor, and occupier of the house, organised such details. He looked up the references in the New Testament to the qualifications of an Elder - in Timothy and Titus. He decided these must be the criteria, not just the best person in their group for the position, but only a leader who met the New Testament standard would be the right man to appoint. In the context of the church fellowship they were completely honest and open with each other. All seemed unanimous in their choice of Ron Bailey. There was some doubt about a co-leader, but after a further three months all doubts were removed and Haydn Jones was the choice. The two were recognised as leaders at a special service attended by Norman Meaton, John Carter, leader of a house church at Manchester, and Derek Harrison. There was no laying on of hands, that seems to have sacramental connotations. They simply prayed for each other.

The church outgrew the meeting room, and they received planning permission to build an extension. This also involved permission for a change in use of premises for the house to be used for religious meetings.

In retrospect Ron Bailey appears to have moved into a church which had a history of bad relationships between the Elders and the Pastor. It is

55

difficult to understand why that fact did not become apparent during his final
year at Birmingham Bible Institute whilst he was helping in the church in a
part time capacity.

Subsequently he seems to have had some hesitation in practising the role
of minister, which role he now seems to have accepted. The present house
church evolved when after considerable thought Ron Bailey elected to follow
the influence of Mr G.W. North rather than the pattern of the Harvestime
Churches. He claims to have had a realisation of the New Birth teaching
independently of Mr North. One wonders whether this is, a) to stress this
particular teaching as direct divine revelation or, b) to minimise Mr North's
personal influence over churches which obviously follow his teaching.

The church has now settled down to a steady pattern of church life
typical of the North fellowships. It is characterised by friendly, caring
relationships.

The Influence of the Church at South Chard

The International Students House Fellowship, Great Portland
Street, London (10)

The International Students House is a large busy residential club catering for students of all nationalities. The ISH Fellowship, as it is known,
owes its name to the fact that its founders, two women, both work in the
club; one is the welfare officer. It owes its continuance if not its
foundation to the help and support of the church at South Chard.

The fellowship consists largely of people who have little existing
church loyalty: students who are in London for a few years, young doctors,
medical students and research students,who are working in London but who
have no friends, family or any connections there. A large percentage of
individuals such as these form part of the ISH Fellowship.

Although the fellowship now functions as a church, its members are
different from the normal church composition as they are nearly all single
people, the only family being that of one of the leaders.

The fellowship was started in the home of Elizabeth Ware. She feels
her background was very influential in forming her attitude to worship and
fellowship. She was brought up in a house church run by her father and it
was his example and teaching that formed the major influence in her life.

Her father had left an exclusive Brethren sect at an early age and only
on his marriage had he resumed an interest in religious activity. He and
his wife, an Anglican, decided to worship in their home rather than attend
church. They saw that Christians in the New Testament met in homes and felt
it was the logical and obvious thing to do. At no time did the house church
become very large. It was mainly composed of the family and the people living
with them together with a few friends who lived near. Although the house
church was completely independent, Elizabeth's father had many friends amongst
Evangelicals of different persuasions. He was greatly encouraged by the

writings of Watchman Nee, who wrote about the patterns of early church life.
Because he was grieved over the divisions of Christendom he neither wanted to
start a movement nor join a denomination. Usually the numbers in his church
were around twenty.

When she was baptised in the Spirit in 1971, an experience unknown in
her father's church, Elizabeth Ware found that real unity lay in the Holy
Spirit, not in doctrine. Previously she had begun to attend meetings
arranged by the Fountain Trust. When she saw the obvious joy in the lives
of the participants she felt very challenged. She had always considered that
in her father's house church they had the ideal situation. When a friend,
Joy Paine from South Chard, came to visit, she took Elizabeth to a house
church in Teddington. (Later this became the Kingston Fellowship.) At this
church she was baptised in the Spirit, and she realised this church was
moving in an area of which her father's group knew nothing. This was a
completely new experience and way of life.

Together with her companion, Elisabeth Collins, she began to attend the
house church at Teddington. She felt at home there and was greatly encouraged.
She began to take car loads of friends, many of whom entered into the experience of the Baptism in the Spirit. Then one day the leaders of the group
suggested that she and her friends should have their own meeting in the flat
in which she and Elisabeth Collins shared.

They began to meet on Wednesday evenings. Immediately the meetings
were popular - the flat was crowded and the worship became very noisy. All
denominations were represented, including some Catholics, and many different
nationalities would be present. However, the two women began to worry that
their neighbours would not appreciate the loud singing and banging of
tambourines.

Eventually, as they were concerned about the noise (the flat is situated in the basement of a quiet terrace bordering Regents Park), they booked
a hall belonging to the Leprosy Mission. They visited Chard and arranged
that Mr Sidney Purse should come as the guest speaker for the first meeting.
On that occasion he preached on the theme of the challenge of following Christ.

After the meeting a number returned to the flat, where another, informal
meeting took place. Elizabeth Ware had shared with Mr Purse their fears that
the meetings were so noisy. In the way he conducted the meetings he showed
her that a meeting which is genuinely "moving in the Spirit" is not unduly
noisy.

The challenge of Mr Purse's preaching had its effect. Numbers decreased.
After three weeks he suggested no more meetings would be arranged for a further three weeks while they prayed and decided what future policy should be.
After that time they began again to meet in the flat, but this time there was
a difference. The meetings were quieter and more spiritual.

By 1974 it became obvious that there was a need for a Sunday meeting.
Here was a problem. The two women had never considered themselves as leaders,
but merely as those who supplied the meeting place. They asked Mr Purse for
advice.

The church at South Chard appears to have an open view about the position of women (although there are no female leaders at Chard). Certainly the Elders at Chard had been happy for the two women to arrange meetings up to this point. However, now the question of Sunday meetings was raised, it was felt that as there were no senior men in the fellowship it would be advisable for them to join a larger group. Accordingly Mr Purse advised them to join the house church at Richmond(11) which was just starting, until such time that God sent them male leaders for the London meeting.

At that time Elizabeth Ware read what she felt was a promise from God in the book of Job:

> "For there is hope for a tree
> If it be cut down, that it will sprout again,
> And that its shoots will not cease." (Job 14:7)

She felt the tree referred to their fellowship and that one day it would be restored.

When the change had been made and they joined the new church at Richmond Elizabeth found that she enjoyed being part of a larger house fellowship. She feels this was an important time in her life, one aspect being that she gained a new vision of what the church is, that without the right spiritual leadership disastrous mistakes could be made.

In the Autumn of 1976 Nick West came onto the scene. He had heard about the prayer meeting the two women held on Thursday mornings. He immediately felt at home with the group who met to pray. As he had no commitments (his parents are farming in Africa), he decided to live for a year at the club before going to University. Then he decided to take a degree in sociology at the nearby Bedford College.

Between 1976 and 1978 there were again evening meetings on Thursdays in the flat of the two women. Then John Badkin, his wife and family joined them. John Badkin had been the leader of a house church in Southgate, North London. He seemed the obvious person to assume a position of authority.

In October 1978 Sunday meetings began. Once a month an outside speaker is invited. At Easter 1979 most of the members of the church went to South Chard for a weekend.

These are early days for this church. Not all the members of the Richmond house church thought they were ready to assume the responsibility of an independent church, and the situation has not been without its tensions. It is an unusual situation, but with the encouragement from Chard it is most likely that the young, enthusiastic fellowship will flourish. In her account, Elizabeth Ware was very conscious of the fact that she, the prime instigator of the church, was a woman. She seems to rely heavily on the much younger Nick West and it is obvious that had not he and John Badkin arrived to function as male leaders the fellowship would not have resumed its independent existence.

This group answers a need for a place of worship for the floating population of London's student and professional world, which offers closer ties of fellowship than would a traditional denominational church.

Again in this chapter I have obtained my information by personal interview, but this has also been reinforced by personal observation, both of the worship meetings and the day to day life of the church. The period of observation has varied from a brief visit to the International Students House Fellowship to a period of one year of the Solihull Christian Fellowship and five years of the Church of the Way, Chester, and Russell House Fellowship, Leamington Spa.

CHAPTER 4: Life in the House Church

Of the three types of house church, that of the largest and most rapidly
expanding, the Harvestime Group, has the most detailed structure and concept
of what the church should be.

Looking at the structure of the church as envisaged by Bryn Jones and
his associates it is seen to be a distinct strand of the Charismatic Movement
which became noticeable in the decade of the sixties. This particular strand
has its roots in Wales, but that is the only affinity it has to Welsh Protestantism. The question which has occupied the minds of Bryn Jones and his colleagues has been, on what authority do they base their ideas of what is the
church and - like other Protestant fundamentalist bodies - their answer is
the Scriptures. Examination of the Scriptures to see where and how the Holy
Spirit operated in the early Christian Church points to the problem of tradition. The early Christian Church broke with the traditions of Judaism. It
appears that religious trappings and the accruement of tradition have to be
swept away before God can work in his Church today. Therefore back in the
Welsh community of Aberdare many could not understand these new ideas which
permitted the buying of ice cream on Sunday, the perusal of Sunday newspapers
or the partaking of a glass of dinner wine.

The emphasis of the movement lies in the concept of the church.(1) The
question is posed: "Are denominations right?" If they are then there is no
problem; if not, then they should cease. To the accusation that they themselves are forming yet another denomination is given the reply that a denomination must have a central governing body, whereas the only link between their churches is a personal one, that of an Apostolic and Prophetic
ministry, which is exercised by these leaders, from many different places,
moving and travelling amongst the churches.

Their concern is the Government of God which is seen in the expression
of the Kingdom of God on earth which is the church. The structure and
authority of the church are seen in personal relationships of members to
each other in the local church, and of leaders to each other across the network. These relationships are based upon the mutual submission of leaders
to leaders, and the submission of church members to those placed in authority
over them. The term used to refer to such submission is "related".

To examine the structure of the church more closely the hierarchy is
composed of church members, then Elders, then Apostles, then God. Hence
the widespread use of the nickname the Pyramid Movement. This hierarchy
is based upon an interpretation of Acts 13:1-3:

"Now in the church at Antioch there were prophets and teachers...
while they were worshipping the Lord and fasting, the Holy Spirit
said, 'Set apart for me Barnabas and Saul for the work to which I
have called them'. Then after fasting and prayer they laid hands
on them and sent them off."

An Apostle is one who is sent out with a specific purpose which is usually to establish a church or to ground in faith a particular group of Christians. There are several people who rank as Apostles in the movement - originally these were the founder members whose numbers will increase as the movement expands. Individual leaders do not call themselves Apostles, but by virtue of establishing and visiting churches they come to be recognised as such. When a man, through his work, receives such recognition, then the church recognises his ministry as an Apostle by the Laying on of Hands. This is not seen as an institution to an office, but rather as a confirmation of what God has been saying through the man's work.

Each Apostle has an apostolic team, who are closely related to each other and to those fellowships with whom they work. Contrary to a first impression there is not an emphasis on rank or order, rather of relationships which are deeply personal. The apostolic teams are obviously formed to facilitate communications across the country, as every local church is visited regularly by an Apostle. The teams are to a certain extent local-ised - Bryn Jones, before he left for the States, headed a team which cov-ered the North East and the Midlands, Arthur Wallis the West Country, Terry Virgo the South of England and John Noble London and the Home Counties. Sometimes two Apostles visit two local churches quite near each other - it is a question of personal relations rather than organisation. Twice a year the apostolic teams meet in conference.

From the Apostles come the teaching themes so that every church receives the same teaching message. There is an awareness that in the past Revivals have faded or developed into a system. Accordingly there is a concern to present a continually challenging message, to show that God is constantly saying something fresh to his people.

The ministry of the church is based on an interpretation of 1 Corinth-ians 12:28:

> "And God has appointed in the church first apostles, second
> prophets, third teachers, then workers of miracles, then
> healers, helpers, administrators, speakers in various kinds
> of tongues."

The ministers in the church are declared to be divinely appointed.

A departure is seen in the recognised practice in denominational churches of a man offering himself for the ministry, undergoing some form of selection and then a period of training before ordination to his work. It is believed that an individual cannot decide for himself; his ministry will become apparent in the fellowship of the local church. The Elders will want to see a man prove himself within the fellowship, his ministry will be encouraged in every way, as it is recognised and more and more opportunities will be given for it to be used and developed.(2)

Another key passage on which the ministries of the church are based is Ephesians 4:11 and 12:

> "And his gifts were that some should be apostles, some prophets,
> some evangelists, some pastors and teachers, for the equipment
> of the saints, for the work of ministry, for building up the
> body of Christ."

62

Gifts of an individual are usually recognised in the context of the meeting, often as a man shows he possesses one or more of the spiritual gifts listed in 1 Corinthians 12:8-10:

> "To one is given through the Spirit the utterance of wisdom,
> and to another the utterance of knowledge according to the same
> Spirit, to another faith by the same Spirit, to another gifts of
> healing by the one Spirit, to another the working of miracles,
> to another prophecy, to another the ability to distinguish
> between spirits, to another various kinds of tongues, to another
> the interpretation of tongues."

Such gifts are recognised in the fellowship and welcomed - but it is also expected that such men will also spend a good deal of their time in Biblical study. No formal theological training is envisaged, and it is also maintained that if a man has a ministry it is a gift from God for the church, his own church, where he will remain until he is mature enough to be asked to shepherd other groups. Then as he spends more time travelling other new Elders will be encouraged to take his place in the home church whilst he is away. In this way new groups receive the immediate encouragement of a visiting experienced Elder, and there are always opportunities for new Elders to emerge in the home church. A distinct anti-clerical atmosphere is felt in the determination to appoint only those who seem obvious spiritual leaders to the role of Elder, the emphasis that an individual does not offer himself, he is recognised. An emphasis which was first declared in this country by Dr Ern Baxter at the summer conference of 1975 as he repeatedly compared the appointment of the denominational churches with the divine appointments of the house churches, illustrated in Scripture by the democratic election of King Saul contrasted with the divine choice of King David.

Within the framework of the local church are two or three Elders depending on the size of the church. Every Elder carries out the function of a shepherd. When an individual or a family become committed to a church the Elders are invited to share in the personal and family lives of the members; in return the Elders are available for counsel and advice. This is the most personal aspect of life in the house church. Although there is great emphasis laid on the family unit and each family follows its own lifestyle, nevertheless it is open to comments and suggestions from the Elders. This two-way process of counsel and advice, exhortation and rebuke is intended to bring about the Biblical pattern of life which is lived according to the will of God. It is never intended there should be any critical or dictatorial methods used - the process of shepherding, as this is known, is described as a deepening of relationships.

Where the advice which is offered is not accepted by the individual or couple concerned there follows what is termed "confrontation" when the matter is discussed from every point of view. It is here that the love of a fellowship is tested; when that love is real the matter is solved without any dissension - when it is weak a serious disagreement could ensue which could and does lead to the "rebellious" leaving the fellowship.(3)

It is this question of submission that has raised the strongest opposition and criticism amongst charismatic circles. More particularly in the United

States, but also echoed in this country, the whole principle of shepherding and the act of submitting one's life to another has been soundly condemned.

But it does seem that many welcome the availability of the Elders, not only for consultation in spiritual matters, but in problems such as the raising of children, marriage guidance and other practical issues which arise from the pressures of modern society.

The principle of submission in church affairs is reflected in family life. The husband is the head of the household - it is interesting this is held to apply universally, not just in church families, so that a woman who is married to a man who is not a church member is counselled to obey him in all things to the extent of not attending church. All decisions in family life are to be made by the husband. Men on the other hand are commanded to be both protective and considerate of their wives and it is stressed that domination plays no part in a Christian marriage. The discipline of children like all other matters is ultimately the responsibility of the father, so that a wife has much of the strain that many present day wives and mothers carry, taken off her, as the husband assumes a responsible caring role. As church life has developed there have been signs of a more relaxed attitude to women, in that it now seems to be accepted that some women may work part-time. Originally it was stressed a wife and mother should be at home. This I understand had to be modified as more professional men joined the churches whose wives had successful careers.

Each church is autonomous, the relationships held to Apostles and Elders are personal and do not involve day to day organisation of the churches. Nevertheless there is a similarity of pattern in the organisation and day to day life of the local churches.

The overall aim is to provide for the needs of every member of the church, both married and single, every age range from babyhood upwards. Although it is noticeable that as a young movement there are relatively few elderly people to be considered. There have been few funerals as yet.

As these churches have expanded many have acquired premises which are large enough to provide social and religious activities for the community. For example at Bradford, the use of Church House illustrates how the church aims to provide for every aspect of life for the individual member. The house is basically on three floors although the design, using a mezzanine arrangement, gives rooms on six levels.

In the basement is a gymnasium for youth activities. There are club activities for teenagers, first aid and car maintenance classes, knitting sessions, classes for prospective brides in sewing and cookery, and classes for prospective fathers in baby care. Also in the basement is the recording studio, for different gospel groups as well as the efficient recording and copying of sermons given at meetings and conferences. A baptistry has been constructed for baptism services, which formerly were held in a local river in summer and an indoor public swimming pool in winter.

On another level is a sleeping nursery for young babies and a creche for toddlers. Those in the fellowship who are qualified nurses take it in turns to care for the children. There is a network of babysitters who release parents to attend the midweek events at the church.

On the ground floor is the shop, which stocks pottery, glassware, wooden crafts, toys and greeting cards which will provide a greater profit than the Christian literature, which is displayed very unobtrusively. Adjoining the shop is a coffee shop and restaurant, above which, connected by a pulley lift, is a kitchen.

The first floor is a block of offices for the Elders and the Secretary of the church. The main auditorium is on the top floor, a large room, which is furnished in light oak with orange curtains, a dais at one end of the room for the speaker, and bright orange stacking chairs; careful floral arrangements complete the impression of good taste. Close circuit television transmits the service to the overflow room, for the church has already outgrown its largest room. This church is licensed for weddings. In other local churches a variety of arrangements occurs. Some couples are married in the local Registrar's office and a religious service is held at a different time. Others ask the Registrar to be present at the service; sometimes a church is hired for the occasion, especially if the group normally meets in a house.

In Bradford once a month the members meet for an agape feast. During the week there are various devotional classes. In the six months of June to December 1978 fifty-six people attended a new converts class; none of these had any previous church connections.

In 1979 the church in Bradford numbered four hundred and twenty-three committed members. Each of these had attended the Commitment Class for ten weeks and then made the decision to become totally committed to the church. The Commitment Classes deal with every aspect of living in the Kingdom of God, such as the fundamental doctrines that every Pentecostal group holds of conversion, water baptism, spirit baptism, followed by the principles of tithing of income, the ethical standards of honesty in business life, and the necessity of submission in every area of life to the Elders of the church. Following the decision of commitment the member is then attached to a house group.

Following the example of Acts 6:3, "Therefore brethren, pick out from among you seven men of good repute, full of the spirit and of wisdom, whom we may appoint to this duty" (of administration), seven men have been appointed to have the responsibility of seven areas of administration. These areas are:

1. Finance - that is the tithe given by church members. The annual sum is £50,000. It is used to support missionaries abroad, travelling ministers and the poor at home and abroad.

2. The Offerings - the people are taught that giving only begins after the tithe has been deducted from the income. The offerings amount to £28,000 per annum. This is used for the upkeep of Church House - electricity, heating and renovations.

3. Health Visitors - these are a team who visit the sick, and those with small babies. Each House Group has a health visitor, some of whom have the appropriate professional qualifications. Any social need of any member is referred to the health visitor. A woman heads this team.

4. Catering - for church functions; the organisation of such events as agape feasts. A woman heads this team.

5. Children's Work - is concerned with those from five to twelve. After twelve years all children participate in the adult meetings. Sunday School instruction is for the children of church members only - it is not open to any other child unless visiting the church with parents. A scheme of work is used which necessitates the child completing assignments at home with the help of parents. Any child who has not completed the work by the following Sunday is an indication to the Elders that the parents have not been conscientious and the situation is investigated. The aim of the Sunday School is to round off what the parents have taught the child during the week.

6. Stewarding - a team of ten stewards are needed each Sunday for the services.

7. The Youth Programme - this covers the young people of thirteen to fifteen years. It consists of written material based on a scheme by an American, Bill Gothead, who writes for a well-known evangelical writer Selwyn Hughes. Leisure activities for this group include camping and mountaineering.

Naturally other smaller churches cannot provide the wealth of facilities offered by the Bradford church. However, in each is seen a general pattern - first the attendance at Commitment Classes and the necessity of making a decision to be committed to the church. Secondly, following such a decision, the designation to a House Group where the newcomer is closely integrated into the fellowship. Thirdly there is the provision of activities, a particular emphasis on children's work, practical help given in decorating and upkeep of members' homes. In short, all aspects of social contact are catered for in the church community.

There is a strong feeling that it is absolutely necessary to maintain cordial working relationships with other churches and individuals who are "moving with God", that is those involved in the current charismatic renewal. In October 1978 the first meeting of charismatic leaders from all the historic denominations was held at a Church of England Conference Centre, Lindley Lodge, Nuneaton. No doubt this move was to counteract an early impression of exclusivism which was apparent in the early formation of the house churches. Now speakers from the denominational churches are invited to speak, particularly at the Celebration Evenings which are regular bi-monthly meetings held in most local churches for all Christians in the surrounding area. In September 1979 the Revd David McInnes, an Anglican minister, was the speaker at a Celebration Evening held by the Solihull Christian Fellowship. Local churches are now anxious to join in inter-church activities provided they are of an evangelical nature.

The Harvestime Group appeals mainly to the middle class professional who appreciates an intellectual content in the preaching. It is noticed that there is an absence of the traditional Gospel-type sermon. Here is a fundamental difference from the denominational evangelical churches, where the church is a place where the Gospel is preached so that souls might be saved, or a pond in which to fish, as Jesus promised his servants would be fishers of men. Those in this group of churches maintain the church is made up of the redeemed, those who are Christians, who have left the world.

To preserve the freshness of the teaching different themes are constantly introduced - both at the annual conference and as the Apostles visit their churches. In the early years of 1973-74, the emphasis was on family life: the submission of a wife to a husband; next came the submission of children to parents and the importance of corporal punishment. In 1976 was the call to become committed to one's local church and for Elders and Pastors to become related with Bryn Jones and his associates. 1978 saw an emphasis on personal witnessing to outsiders, and 1979 brought a further stress on the maturing of the life of the church. Now the church had been gathered together it was time to concentrate on the spiritual maturity both of the group and of in- dividuals.

All this appeals to the young middle class - usually those with growing families. By far the majority of church members are in their thirties - probably because that is the age range of the founder leaders who have tended to gather round them people of a similar age and background.

In that the church at Bradford is at variance, as this is mainly composed of working class people - those with manual occupations, who find housing accommodation one of their biggest problems. As this was where the movement began this fact could account for the earlier attitude to women, in that the Yorkshire lasses of the Bradford church had no aspirations other than acquir- ing a husband and family. As the churches have multiplied, however, it is the graduate and business executives who make up the congregations. In every local church a high proportion of University graduates, medical doctors, industrial executives, solicitors, teachers, nurses and social workers will be found. There is moreover a middle class atmosphere in these churches in that such is the expression of fellowship life that the poorer families are helped in material ways so that there is no inequality among members. Practical aspects of fellowship are so dealt with that there is no self- consciousness of either giving or receiving material gifts. In effect all members are helped to assume a middle class status.

Moving to the second type of house church, those which have arisen from the work of Mr North, one finds a completely different characteristic. Here the emphasis is upon a very distinctive theological interpretation which is known as the New Birth Experience.

Adherents of this particular viewpoint trace its development back to the Protestant Reformation. At the time of the Reformation Luther spoke of Re- generation, by which he meant Conversion and Justification by Faith. Calvin later made a distinction between Regeneration and Conversion, maintaining Regeneration came first, that is unless Regeneration came by a sovereign act of God a person would never turn to God. Sometimes it seems there was a definite place in his thinking for an assurance of salvation, or a sealing of the Holy Spirit.

The Methodists saw a twofold experience. Firstly one is justified by faith, at which time one's record of sin is dealt with and Righteousness imputed to the individual by God. Secondly came the experience of santific- ation by faith, when God removed sin and one had a clean heart; this led on to empowering for service, although the Methodists did not use the terminology of the Baptism in the Spirit.

The Salvation Army originally saw Holiness as a separate experience; their emphasis is not on Pentecostalism but is more relative to a clean heart. This is reflected in the fact that today the morning meeting of the Army is still called the Holiness Meeting.(4)

In the early 20th Century, at one of the first centres of modern Pentecostalism (Azusa Street, Los Angeles, California), W.J. Seymour came to the conclusion as a result of studying the Scriptures that there were three distinct experiences - Regeneration, Sanctification and Baptism in the Spirit. The latter meant power for service.

T.B. Barrett, a Methodist minister, visited Azusa Street and later Sunderland, England, where he met with Alexander Boddy, one of the pioneers of the Pentecostal Movement in Britain. Barrett, and thence the British Pentecostals, believed in three distinct experiences, like Seymour, of Regeneration, Sanctification and Spirit Baptism.

In England many early Pentecostals had a background of Holiness teaching, i.e. they tended to see Holiness or Sanctification as a separate experience, and now Spirit Baptism was a further experience.

In the United States there was a division in the Pentecostal Movement, when W.J. Seymour expelled W.H. Durham from the Apostolic Faith Church, when Durham reduced the three-stage experience to two steps, maintaining sin was dealt with at conversion. Since 1908 this has been an ongoing point of dissension in American Pentecostalism.(5) Those from a Holiness background wanted to emphasise Sanctification as a separate experience, but they became a minority and accordingly it was generally accepted there was no Scriptural justification to demand or expect two experiences to deal with sin, and that Regeneration and Sanctification were the initial experience of one who became a Christian. Today the Assemblies of God Churches in particular are very strong on this twofold experience of first Regeneration/Sanctification and then the Spiritual Baptism.

Later charismatics in Britain have not generally had a Holiness background, more likely they have been drawn from circles influenced by the Keswick Convention or by the ideas of Roy Hession and the Ruanda Revival. In this tradition Conversion/Regeneration is seen as a continual process in the life of a believer, which then in the thought of the charismatic suddenly receives a second crisis experience known as the Baptism in the Spirit.

The chain of fellowships I term Harvestime, together with the charismatics in the denominational churches and the traditional Pentecostals, see a twofold experience of Regeneration which leads onto the Baptism in the Spirit.

Mr North and his co-leaders differ from this view in that they believe the experience of the Baptism in the Spirit encompasses every work or act that God can do in the life of a believer. When a believer experiences this Spirit Baptism he enters into the fulness of life of a "born again" Christian and receives every blessing that God has for him. That is Mr North has further reduced the two-stage pattern to a once-for-all experience which he terms the "New Birth".

This is the point at which other evangelical Christians differ - and the point of contention is the term "born again". Traditionally this is based on the words of Jesus to Nicodemus in John 3 and has meant the decision of an individual to become a Christian, coupled with the knowledge of personal sins forgiven because of the atoning work of Christ on the Cross. Mr North and his followers believe the initial experience of sins forgiven is too inadequate to claim to be New Birth. New Birth only happens when the believer receives the fulness of God, when he begins to live a fully spiritual life; their terminology would be to "walk in the Spirit".

It follows logically that the total regeneration of the believer means that "whosoever is born of God doth not commit sin; for his seed remaineth in him and he cannot sin, because he is born of God" (1 John 3:9). This is the second offence to evangelical churchmen, being seen as a claim to sinless perfection.

Finally Mr North firmly asserts the superiority of the Authorised Version of the Bible maintaining all other versions to be based on texts full of errors!

This second type of house church tends to be much smaller in numbers than the Harvestime Churches, therefore in many cases fellowships still meet in houses. Each is completely autonomous and has no connection with any other group. The sole link is the personal influence of Mr North and a few of his preachers who visit regularly.

It is an interesting point that Mr North is anxious to avoid any semblance of influence, as several of the leaders of different fellowships each claim to have had a simultaneous revelation of the teaching concerning the New Birth, including Ron Bailey of Birmingham, Dave Orange of Leamington Spa and Derek Gitsham of Worcester.

Mr North himself realises he will be accused of heresy, that this is the price of claiming an absolute truth that others have missed. He states there was a great need for Reformation of Christian doctrine and sees the New Covenant of Christ starting at the Day of Pentecost, not on Calvary as most orthodox churches.

These house fellowships tend to have more of an appeal to the lower middle class than do the Harvestime Churches. Although they too have their share of teachers and nurses, there is a content with which the less well educated can identify, such as the widely held view that higher education is unnecessary and superfluous to the teaching of the Bible. Ron Bailey sees a tension between those of a middle class background and the lower middle class or working class which even the friendliness of the house church cannot eradicate. Even such a thing as the offer of a lift home can emphasise the fact that one has a car and the other has not. The difference is marked however the situation is handled, it is the middle class who do all the giving, the working class who are always receiving.

This type of church draws a large number of artisans, plumbers,

electricians and carpenters; Ron Bailey stated ten per cent of his fellowship in Birmingham were unskilled labourers.

In the Leamington Spa fellowship a great deal of the work is directed
at those from working class backgrounds. Many of these who come to the
Oranges' home are those without employment, on probation or from deprived
homes.

The first was a girl called Liz. She was the second of seven children
who became involved with heroin as a young teenager. Her father no longer
wanted her at home because of the reactions of the neighbours to the continual encounters with the police that Liz had. One of her school friends asked
the curate at the Anglican church to help her - and so she came into contact
with the Oranges who were then still in the Anglican church. Frequently Liz
ran away from home, sometimes going as far as London. Dave Orange took her
back home four times after these escapades. Finally he arranged with her
father, who clearly indicated he was reluctant for her to live at home, for
Liz to live with them.

Shortly after Liz visited the police station to confess she had thrown
a brick through a shop window late one night. At the subsequent hearing the
magistrates were so impressed with the evidence of her changed way of life
that she was discharged.

She obtained one of the few places available at the local College of
Further Education on the NNEB course, but she continually refused to return
home at night and would wander about the streets. She smoked and drank
heavily. Then she left and went to London where she was arrested and charged
with vagrancy. The police constable who arrested her was a member of a house
church and contacted Dave Orange, who immediately went to the police station.
After talking with him the police dropped all charges. Eventually Liz
qualified as a nursery nurse. She was unable to obtain work locally, and
so she worked for the Oranges, looking after their young children. During
the time they were in rented accommodation Liz claims to have had a spiritual
experience when "God met and delivered her". Later, after they were established at Russell House, she felt in her heart she had lost touch with God.
She went to Worcester to talk to Derek Gitsham. Later she went out to the
Philippine Islands where she joined a missionary couple for three months,
helping in their work. She returned home, but planned to go back to the
Philippines.

Another case was that of Alan Burman. He used to frequent The Fisherman
coffee bar and was at one time homeless and sleeping rough. Then he obtained
a room and Dave Orange helped him to find work. Penny Orange kept his wages
for him, did his washing and gave him breakfast and tea. He was then con-
victed of selling stolen property and sent to Wolverhampton Prison. Typically
Dave Orange used this opportunity to meet the prison chaplain and obtain permission for members of the fellowship to hold a service for the prisoners.

The Oranges offered to give Burman a home when he was discharged, and
because of this offer he was allowed out of prison on parole. The Oranges
requested that he must be in the house by 11 p.m. and that he must endeavour
to look for work. Burman stayed with the Oranges for four months. At the
end of three months Dave raalised he had no intention of finding work. So

he told Burman if there was no indication at the end of another month that he was seriously trying to obtain work, then he must leave the house. The day before the end of that month Burman disappeared, two weeks later he called to collect his clothes. He went to a home run by the Social Services in Worcester.

Burman's probation officer then approached the Oranges to ask if they would give a home to an eighteen year old girl named Jane. She was an adopted child, who had been in a Community Home, and was on probation for grievous bodily harm inflicted upon another girl. She had attempted to break into her adoptive parents' home; they wanted no contact with her at all. Jane stayed with the Oranges until her case was heard - six weeks, during which time she appeared to settle into the household very well. Both Penny and Dave went to Court to say Jane could live with them. Jane was fined £1 per week and discharged into the care of the Oranges. Three days later she disappeared.(6)

The Oranges see this type of activity as part of the work of their fellowship. Clearly not every one is a success story but illustrates the fact that these fellowships have some appeal for the deprived of society. There is not the emphasis on structure and authority, and a commitment is not demanded of those who attend - indeed, it is recognised some may wish to retain their links with denominational churches. The meetings and the Sunday Schools are open to all; the children's work in particular is viewed as a missionary endeavour in one of the poorer districts of the town.

The sphere of influence of these fellowships does not seem to be so wide as that of the Harvestime Churches. Many of the leaders appear to be physically related. The son of Mr North is leader of a church in Reading, his son-in-law has a church in Walsall. At Worcester Derek Gitsham mentioned his father-in-law led a large fellowship in Exeter.

The adherents of the North fellowships view themselves as standing firmly in the Puritan tradition. They compare themselves with the early Quakers, and with Wesley. In particular much of their worship is based upon the ideas and pattern set forth in Wesley's writings. Their hymn book, "Hymns of Eternal Faith", is a collection of Wesley's hymns. The tone of the worship is Christocentric, the whole emphasis being the desirability for the believer to immerse himself in Christ. The meetings tend to be led by one person, the leader, in contrast to those of Harvestime, where several men always participate. These fellowships are also more exclusive - only men known to subscribe to the theory of the New Birth are invited to speak or lead a meeting. There is virtually no contact with other Christian groups, although this is no doubt due to the attitude of charismatics and evangelicals who see these fellowships as a manifestation of heresy.

The third type of house church, that of South Chard, places the main emphasis of church life on what is termed Body Ministry. That is everyone present in the meetings is free to contribute to the worship. This can be in any form - the delivery of an exhortation, reading a passage of Scripture, a song or an exercise of one of the spiritual gifts such as prophecy, tongues and interpretation, or word of knowledge (1 Corinthians 12:8-10). In this way every member in the church can play a part in the meetings.

This church has several themes to its overall aims, which cover evangelism and Bible teaching. There is also great emphasis laid on healing, which has led to the church becoming well known in Pentecostal circles. The ministry of healing falls into two categories, physical healing and mental.(7)

Very often physical healing takes place during the services, when a member present will have a word of knowledge that someone present is suffering from a certain disease. The word of knowledge can be vague, such as "a pain in the right leg" or more specific, such as "there is someone here who has cancer of the liver". Following the word of knowledge being acknowledged by the sufferer concerned prayer and the laying on of hands takes place. Such occurrences happen during the regular services of the church - there are no specific healing services. Mental and emotional healing is achieved by personal counselling Since the belief is that all sickness is due to demonic influence exorcism is practised.

During the decade of the sixties the church at South Chard became known in evangelical circles for their practice of baptising people in the name of Jesus only rather than in the traditional formula of the Trinity. Much bad feeling was caused, particularly as their efforts were extended to visitors from other churches, not just members of their own community. It is interesting to note that although it was this controversy which prompted Bryn Jones to move to Bradford, the church at South Chard now enjoys good relationships with both other types of house churches. Men from Chard visit churches in the Harvestime group and indeed have been instrumental in the early growth of some, e.g. The Church at Merryfield House, Witney. It is believed the opposing sides have agreed to differ and the church at South Chard is more discreet in regard to baptising those coming from other churches.

In all three types of house church women have no part whatsoever in the leadership - although the church at South Chard would be more sympathetic to the idea of a woman leading and has been known to encourage a church under the leadership of a woman. Nevertheless, in the face of male criticism of a woman leader the leaders at Chard would advise the cessation of female leadership.

At first glance it appears that male superiority is held as a priority; however, the underlying philosophy is that men and women have a different role in life. As every detail of life must be lived according to Biblical principles, Paul's injunctions on women in churches are taken very seriously. Although women are permitted to pray, give a testimony or sing, it would be unthinkable for a woman to preach or lead a Bible study, if men were present. In the practical administration of the churches women do play a part, albeit a subsidiary or supporting one to men.

In comparison the three types of house church are very different. Chard, the first to emerge in the early fifties, has a traditional Pentecostal type of worship, but their meetings have their own characteristics, so that it is quite easy to recognise a house church which has been influenced by South Chard. The most obvious characteristic is the practice of singing a hymn, a chorus, or even one line over and over again. There is no need for the congregation to have hymn books, as everyone knows the words when they have been sung for fifteen to twenty minutes. Tambourines and hand clapping are much in evidence, as in the classic Pentecostal worship.

It is in the worship that the differences between the groups become apparent. In none of the groups is there a set order of service, except in so far that the first hour is occupied by worship, the second hour, or longer, by a sermon, then a brief time of closing worship.

The Chard fellowships are unmistakable with their loud repetitive singing. The meetings of the North fellowships are quieter, and the leader plays an all important part, both leading the worship and delivering the sermon. Music is provided by piano and guitars. The singing is mostly from "Redemption Hymnal" (the Pentecostal hymn book used by both other types of house churches). The long solemn hymns in the Wesley collection "Hymns of Eternal Truth" compiled by Mr North perhaps typify the nature of the worship. There is a strong emphasis on personal holiness and a lack of the exuberance of the other two types of fellowship.

In contrast to the two preceding types, the spontaneous singing led by a group of men together with a backing of piano, drums, cymbals, violins, guitars, flutes and even harps symbolises the character of the Harvestime meetings. These are led not necessarily by the Elders, but by any men who wish to do so - and often by different individuals each week. The music gives a quality to the worship which is most attractive and an informality not found in traditional church music. Many of the songs have a rhythm reminiscent of Jewish folk songs. A feature of this movement is the constant stream of new hymns and choruses which are composed. Each yearly Conference has seen a new pamphlet of hymns many of which are new compositions. This reflects the leaders' concern that the movement will not stagnate or develop traditions but will continue to represent the ongoing restoration of the church. A hint of the strictness exercised in the Harvestime churches is seen in the way the singing is halted if the large congregation at the Conference sing a line incorrectly, and then practise singing it over again before the hymn or chorus is resumed. The individual musical expression of the types of house church brings to the surface the wider divisions between them. It is also noticed in the Conference meetings at Harrogate that messages in tongues are expressly forbidden from the floor of the meeting, and a word of prophecy is only allowed from a member of the congregation if prior permission is sought from the Elders on the platform, when it is then given by the person concerned through the platform microphone. The reason given for this ruling was the bad acoustics of the auditorium; one wonders whether there was an underlying motive of a) preserving order in the large meetings and b) preventing any "messages" being given of which the Elders did not approve. Certainly there is a complete lack of any Pentecostal disorder in the meetings at the Conference, which is efficiently organised with close-circuit TV in areas where visibility of those on the platform is poor, a translation area for the contingents from non-English speaking countries and an interpreter for the deaf.

Possibly the differences in the churches can be traced to the underlying vision of the types. Chard has the intent of establishing Body Ministry in the Christian Church, the North groups are concerned with the personal holiness of the individual, whereas the Harvestime churches see themselves as an eschatological grouping of God's people.

Very obvious comparisons can be drawn with Bryan Wilson's definitions of a religious sect(8), particularly those under his label of Conversionist sect. Members join a house church voluntarily and membership is conditional upon a heart response to evangelical doctrine, although this response could have happened previously. Although new members are welcomed, the house church is not open in the same way as a denominational church opens twice on Sundays for passers-by, and in the Harvestime group, children's work is restricted to those belonging to church members.

Once an initiated member, the individual must meet constantly the strict requirements of the house church. Any deviation from the moral, ethical or spiritual code is not tolerated - gone is the broad laissez-faire attitude of the denominational churches. Membership of the house church is total not casual. In every type of house church one's personal life is lived out according to standards which are seen to be at variance with the world.

Bryan Wilson has further maintained that the second generation will continue in the sect because to leave would involve loss of identity.(9) Great care is taken to ensure that children are completely integrated into the activities of the group, so that if a child were later to leave he would find himself completely disorientated.

It is very difficult to obtain information on those who have left the house churches, as all members are bound by loyalty to their local church not to discuss matters of dissension. Certainly in the Harvestime churches many have lost their initial enthusiasm as the personal demands of the principles of authority and submission were realised. Goos Vedder mentioned numbers decreased from one hundred to thirty in the early days of his church. One young woman, a nursery school teacher in her early twenties, described how difficult she found it to find her place both in society and church life after leaving. She was a committed member for three years of a Harvestime church but gradually found she was not willing for the Elders to have control over every area of her life. As every decision had to be put before the Elders for their approval she said it seemed as if the Elders were in fact acting as mediators between the people in the church and God, and that no direct contact could be established between an individual and God. Increasingly she found it hard to believe that the Elders were always right and that they always spoke with divine authority. She found it difficult to leave, but eventually broke away, to realise she was without connections of any kind. She found it hard to acclimatise to the more casual, less demanding worship of a denominational church, and tried first a Pentecostal Assembly before she finally joined an Anglican church. Only on leaving did she become aware of how involved every aspect of her life was with the people in the house church.

Thus it can be firmly stated the house church provides an alternative, as does the sect, both in worship and in a total way of life. All three types of house church clearly indicate the establishment of an alternative society.

CHAPTER 5: Historical Comparisons of the House Church Movement with
Early Methodism, Brethrenism and the Early Pentecostals

In considering the implications of the House Church Movement certain
comparisons can be traced with other movements which sought originally to
revive the denominational churches. Movements such as Methodism, Brethren
and the Early Pentecostals all bear some similarities in both concepts and
practices to the present-day House Churches.

Methodism

Methodism marks the last defeat of the Anglican Church's attempt to
retain its monopoly. The Church of England had never entirely succeeded in
its monopolistic attempt - but the end of the eighteenth century heralded
the beginning of our present pluralistic society.

Previously the Church had been weakened by external factors. The
Tudors, that is Henry VIII and Elizabeth I, had established the Church of
England but had used it for their own aims; for example, as the monasteries
were destroyed, both clerical livings and church property passed into the
hands of laymen. As A.D. Gilbert describes the situation:

"The Tudors weakened the church economically while
defending it politically."(1)

The Stuarts undermined this political status by their overt Catholic
sympathies and by the effect on religious practices caused by the resultant
Civil War and Republic. For religion to flourish continuity is essential,
and both Tudor and Stuart policies reacted against the Church in that where
a parish had not had sufficient care, the Church in that area had declined
and the people became apathetic. During the Civil War church attendance
had continued to drop, so that the hold of the Anglican Church over the
people had diminished. The changes brought about by the Commonwealth and
then the Restoration caused many people to abandon their allegiance to the
established Church. Many did not want to acknowledge Episcopacy at the
Restoration and turned to the Dissenting groups.

The Toleration Act of 1689 lowered the status of the Church even further
and under the Whigs the strength of the Dissenters grew. Under Dutch William
and the German Georges the essentially English characteristic of the Anglican
Church disappeared. Conflicts - changes - disruptions - a clergy that were mainly interested in the secular advantages of their position, few concerned with
the devotional life and very few interested in an evangelistic approach - all
these elements contributed to the composition of the 18th century Anglican
Church.

England, therefore, was not efficiently cared for or organised; large
areas were untouched by the Church, apathy was rife and society as a whole
was no longer willing to accept the established Church.

It is not surprising then that the Church did not effect any attempt to
provide for the spiritual needs of the new industrial towns. The social and
economic conditions of these towns created a working class population who
were oblivious of any form of religion. It was to this area that the early

Methodists addressed their concern and their efforts.

The situation in the 20th century bears some comparison, certainly with the established Church. Within the Church of England wide divergences of theological opinion have led to at least three distinct groupings of Evangelical, Liberal and Catholic schools of thought. Widespread secularisation of society has had the result that the local Parish Church has as little relevance to the inhabitants of any town as did its counterpart in the 18th century, although in rural districts the church still fills a place in the community. Amongst the clergy, although the indolence prevalent in the 18th century has disappeared, still many men enter Holy Orders for a career and some with little idea of a personal faith in God. With the onset of secularisation the whole relevance of religion has been called into question; so, as in the 18th century, Christianity touches only a fringe of the population - but for different reasons. Whereas then the mass of people were ignorant and neglected by Churchmen, today people are ignorant of Christianity, not because they have no chance to hear the Gospel, but because they see no point in it - an apathy which stems from uninterest is the mark of the average Englishman today. Mass evangelistic campaigns render little impact of a permanent nature on society; man prefers the immediate, material rewards of the technological age. The effects of the Copernican Revolution have been, that not only is man no longer the centre of God's world, but that God has no place or relevance in man's society. Man is completely secular, but with that secularity has come an independence which merges into anonymity. The secular society does not cater for man's emotional, or spiritual needs. Accordingly in cities in particular there occur arid deserts of loneliness where crime, mental illness and suicide attempts are high. A situation not so different from the 18th century in that material misery has been replaced by spiritual - and in each a new form of contact with the masses was required.

Wesley brought a new message - in a new way - to the industrial poor. A message which was to bring them self-respect and to many a self-industriousness which would eventually lead to prosperity.

Today the house church brings an alternative form of society to an anonymous computerised people. Many join wanting friends, and simply to have a sense of belonging. The nuclear age brought a worldwide sense of insecurity and the house church offers an assurance of belonging, to God and his ultimate plans for the world, and to the warm fellowship of the company of His people on earth.

One important difference between the eighteenth century and the twentieth is that today religion is a personal matter, of concern only to the individual. In the eighteenth century religion was still closely linked with the political scene.

After the hopes of a Catholic Restoration finally diminished after 1688, as the Whig power increased they were not so concerned about religious uninterest amongst the people as about an established Church which was largely Tory and partly Jacobite. Accordingly it was expedient to introduce a Toleration Act which brought into official religion the first move towards a pluralistic society. Then, as the Anglican Church was consolidated into the fabric of society, as the link between Squire and Parson was cemented - both Catholic and Dissenter became aware that they were both simply part of a minority group. The Catholic knew there was no hope of a Catholic monarch after the final defeat of the Stuart cause in 1745. The number of influential dissenting families had diminished after the Restoration of Charles II, so that the Anglican Church remained securely part of the Hanoverian political settlement.

Within the Anglican framework from 1678 and increasingly after 1690 voluntary religious societies appeared. Some such as John Sharp, Archbishop of York, in 1699 saw the inherent dangers in such meetings to the established Church: "...some time or other we may feel ill consequences from them".(2) Those participating in the meetings of the voluntary societies felt their parochial loyalties would be strengthened and local clergy encouraged. It is however certain that many of the early Methodists came from the ranks of the religious societies.

Similarly it is from the ranks of the charismatic house groups and prayer meetings that many today have emerged to swell the ranks of the house church. Whether the opposition comes from a minister, prominent church members or simply the frustrations of church tradition, there comes a point when it is realised the existing church system - be it Anglican or Free Church - is unlikely to be renewed.

With any voluntary grouping formed within an existing structure there is an implicit if not explicit protest against that structure. It is an attempt to improve or rectify deficiencies in the existing organisation, although the point at which such groups finally separate can vary according to circumstances; eventually however such a group will either separate or disintegrate.

John Wesley had a policy:

"...go always, not only to those that want you, but to those that want you most."(3)

So a Methodist society would emerge in parishes which were most neglected. Today there is a marked contrast in that house churches are often formed in areas where there is intense spiritual activity and the nucleus will be a group of experienced Christians, not those newly brought into the faith. Also it is not the neglected poor who form the group but successful professional and business members of society - the majority are married couples with young children, families at the peak of their enjoyment of life. Methodism began as a means of bringing the Gospel to those not likely to hear it in a church situation. On the part of John Wesley it was an oft repeated intention ro revive the Church. Those involved in the House Church Movement see this as an answer to the failure to revive the Church. They will maintain that only by leaving the denominational structures will it be possible for people to experience living in the Kingdom of God, in other words: new wine must have new wineskins. In 1755 the issue of separation from the Church was discussed by the Conference for three days, so that the question of separation of those who feel they have some new revelation or experience from God is not a new thing. Today there are those (G.W. North among them) who firmly assert that in every generation there is a different spiritual phenomenon which necessitates a further fragmentation of the Church. Methodism broke the monopoly of the Church of England. Since that time a multiplication of sects has ensued. Churchmen see the House Church Movement as yet another weakening of

77

the Establishment. It is interesting to note that when Wesley himself des-
paired of reviving the Anglican Church he placed the reason not on the numbers of apathetic or hostile clergy but clearly on the fact that evangelical
clergy who supported Methodism were too inhibited by the strictures of the
system to be able to support or encourage Methodist societies in their midst.
This is exactly the reason the house church leaders will give as to why they
cannot be part of a denominational church - that although they will work
closely with charismatic churches nevertheless they maintain the clergy are
too enmeshed in the system to identify with what the house church advocates
as the present restoration of God's people.

George Whitfield, then John Wesley and the early Methodist preachers,
pioneered the techniques of mass evangelism. Yet it was because churches
were closing to them that the original sermon in the open air was delivered
on a hillside at Kingswood, Bristol, on 17th February, 1739. As the established Church closed its pulpits so the Methodist preachers used fields,
hills, often barns or warehouses. The early societies which emerged met in
homes, in the kitchens of farmhouses and cottages, then as numbers grew the
little groups transferred to larger accommodation, in smithys, shops, or work-
sheds. The struggle to build permanent premises was intensified by the fact
that as long as they remained part of the Church of England the benefits con-
ferred on Dissenters by the Toleration Act (1689) did not apply to them, and
they could be, and sometimes were, prosecuted under the Conventicles Acts
(1664 and 1670). The 18th century, at the onset of the Industrial Revolution,
was the age in which mass evangelism could reach the poor. The 20th century
by contrast is approaching the age whereby man is learning to use technology
so that we are entering the age of leisure. Leisure pursuits assume greater
importance, therefore one of the most successful methods of promoting a
message or an idea is through the medium of a Conference holiday - a medium
which the Harvestime churches have used to the fullest extent. It has been
claimed that the personal outworking of their faith so affected the early
Methodists that in the second half of the 18th century there were no happier
homes in England than those of the first Methodists. No doubt a sweeping
statement made in retrospect from the 20th century - but nevertheless Methodist teaching began to penetrate the prevailing ignorance concerning the child,
seeking both to educate and give physical care to poor children and to show
some affection and spiritual provision. It was the start of children being
considered and viewed in their own right and seen no longer as imperfect
adults. Such steps were taken slowly and viewed with 20th century understanding seem primitive. Children at the Foundery School from the age of
six years were present at the morning service at 5 a.m. They worked from
6 a.m. to midday and from 1 to 5 p.m. If absent without leave for two days
in any week they were asked to leave. Yet at that time this severe routine
opened up new horizons for the children of the poor. They were fed and
clothed by the women of the society - within a short time they were literate
and fit to learn a trade. Wesley recognised the importance of securing the
following generation, and although his methods today seem questionable a clear
similarity is seen in the attitudes and techniques employed by the children's
workers in the house churches.

Firstly in all types of house church a strong emphasis is placed upon
family life, in which children play a clearly defined role. The Harvestime
churches ·in particular pay serious attention to the needs of children. In
the church situation much thought and care is given to the work in the Sunday

Schools - which follows the same themes as in the adult preaching. At Conferences the children's meeting times are viewed, not as a means of occupying the children so that parents are free to attend their meeting, but as the focal point of an important part of the Conference work.

The firm belief is that the strength of the community lies in the security of marriage and family life. Thus individual families often stand in contrast to others in their neighbourhood and, although church families are not immune to stresses and problems, nevertheless they appear to surmount these, supported as they are by the help of the local church members. This presents an attractive aspect of church life to outsiders and observers.

Thus, in comparison, 18th century Methodism gave a self-respect and a desire for improvement to the working classes - today the security the house church offers gives a fresh stability to the institution of marriage and family life, which is fast becoming obsolete in secular society.

Methodists became well known for their social concern. As yet no comparable interest has emerged from the House Churches apart from a co-operation with such organisations as TEAR fund and the donating of quite large sums of money to the Third World countries. One evening collection at the Dales Bible Week Annual Conference at Harrogate of the Harvestime Churches is always sent to the underprivileged in the Third World. This collection will amount to a figure around £10,000.

A further comparison is seen between the early bands of Methodism and the home groups of the Harvestime Churches. As soon as several members in a community emerged they were joined together in a band in order to learn and experience Christian fellowship. Based on the Moravian groups Wesley had seen in Georgia, these formed the initial move towards the ultimate separation from the established Church.

When the numbers of bands grew so that the Wesley brothers could no longer personally supervise, John Wesley compiled the written requirements of membership. Eleven questions were asked of newcomers before they were admitted, thereafter five questions were to be answered by each member each week(5):

1. What known sins have you committed since our last meeting?

2. What temptations have you met with?

3. How were you delivered?

4. What have you thought, said, or done of which you doubt whether it be sin or not?

5. Have you nothing you desire to keep secret?

The bands were made up of those who knew they had experienced forgiveness of personal sins. Later by 1744 the select societies had emerged whose members, elected from the bands, had progressed so that they "walked in the light of God".(6)

No such progression is seen in the modern house groups - rather the meetings are arranged solely to preserve the advantages of meeting in a small group as the churches grow larger, although in the Harvestime Churches admittance to a house group is conditional upon graduation from a commitment class. The openness of shared lives in the intimate circle of the house group gives a similar result to the more formal questions of the band meeting.

An echo of the Wesleyan emphasis on personal assurance and piety is a conscious development of the teaching in the North Churches. In the Harvestime Churches the aim is to develop the activities of the church - as a group of families experiencing living in the Kingdom of God, worshipping, helping and sharing with each other in practical ways.

In 1752 the idea of the class meeting emerged; originally it was a plan to gather together to repay the debt on the preaching house in Bristol - one penny each person - the richer pledging to make up the deficit of the poorer members. Here the idea of the Methodist family came about - the class was open to all and was to make a contribution to the growth of Methodism far beyond the original intention of providing the money to pay for one preaching house. Wesley saw the potential - as those appointed to collect the pennies learnt of family troubles and tragedies. Here was a ready made system of personal care by Elders who would encourage and admonish the members. Such close contact and concern has been developed by both the North and the Harvestime groups, although both in different ways.

John Wesley describes(7) how travelling through "one of the pleasantest parts of England to Hawley", Yorkshire, he discovered the landlord had evicted all the Methodists from their homes. So they had built some houses on the outskirts of the town and between forty and fifty were living there. This is a pattern which is often followed today. Some families purchase a large house and live there together on semi-community lines, whilst preserving the unity of the individual family structure. Such a venture is Merryfield House at Witney. Frequently several families in a church will buy houses in the same road.

Perhaps one of the most obvious comparisons between the early Methodists and the House Church Movement is the prolific writing of hymns and songs. But Charles Wesley wrote for an uneducated illiterate people - words which as they were learnt by heart would teach them the elements of the Christian faith:

> "Long my imprisoned spirit lay,
> Fast bound in sin and nature's night.
> Thine eye diffused a quickening ray.
> I woke, the dungeon filled with light.
> My chains fell off, my heart was free.
> I rose, went forth and followed thee."

The emphasis on personal assurance of a changed life is obvious.

Although the adherents of the House Churches are both literate and educated they likewise sing their theology:

> "How lovely on the mountains are the feet of Him
> Who brings good news, good news;
> Proclaiming peace, announcing news of happiness.
> Our God reigns, our God reigns. (repeated several times)
> Ends of the Earth see the salvation of your God

Jesus is Lord, is Lord.
Before the nations He has bared His holy arm,
Your God reigns, your God reigns. (repeated several times)

The Brethren

It is a significant fact that many of the leaders and members of the
House Church Movement in both the North Churches and the Harvestime have
come into the movement from Brethren Assemblies. From the early days of
Brethrenism there has been a resistance and a reserve felt against the
phenomenon of speaking in tongues - this stemmed from a reaction to the
Irving movement which was an early contemporary of Brethrenism. At that
time speaking in tongues was allied to the heretical Christology of Irving
himself.

The first point of interest is the fact that the Brethren would own no
name or title. They saw in the New Testament a pattern of local neighbourhood churches. This corresponds exactly to the House Churches. Neither
group has a name - each local church has its own name, but there is no overall title or indication which will connect it with any other church or individual. This is a deliberate attempt to avoid the accusation of forming
a new denomination. The pioneers of the Brethren movement felt they could
accept no title which could not apply to all God's people. Hence, they
became known as the brethren, which later was spelt with a capital letter.

Between 1812 and 1820 certain Christians in New York corresponded, expressing dissatisfaction with the church situation and expressing a desire
for a Scriptural fellowship. In other parts of the world, British Guyana in
South America, and Rangoon, India, similar letters were exchanged so that
this was a movement which appeared spontaneously in different areas. The
movement emerged due to the activity of seven men(8): Edward Cronin, Edward
Wilson, H. Hutchinson, William Stokes, J. Parnell (later Lord Congleton),
J.C. Bellett and John N. Darby. It can be seen as a reaction against early
Biblical criticism and also against the Tractarian movement on the one hand
and the Irvingites on the other.

Edward Cronin was the first to take steps, although Ironside points out
that Bellett and Darby had independently been thinking the same way.(9)

Cronin was born a Catholic; later he experienced an evangelical conversion. He went to Dublin for health reasons, and there qualified as a
doctor. It puzzled Cronin why Christ's Church should be so divided: he
felt denominationalism was wrong. Here he stands as a direct counterpart
to the House Church leaders who hold the same strong conviction. Cronin also
saw in the Bible no evidence for a one man ministry in the Church.

As he was a convert from Catholicism all the Protestant churches welcomed
him as a visitor, but when he became resident in Dublin he was informed that
he must become a member of a particular church in order to be accepted as one
of the community. He joined an Independent Church in York Street, but this
eventually upset him and he tended to spend the hours of divine service in
the countryside meditating. Finally he was condemned from the pulpit.

One of the deacons of the church objected and he also left. The two men began to meet together to break bread. When Wilson, the deacon, later went to England two female cousins of Cronin who had also left York Street Independent Church because of sympathy for their cousin, and a bookseller named Timms joined him, and these four met to break bread together regularly. In 1827 Darby and Bellett and Stokes joined them, and as the tiny meeting grew larger Mr Hutchinson offered them a larger room in Fitzwilliam Square.

It was a group of evangelical malcontents from different denominations who gathered at 9, Fitzwilliam Square one Sunday in November 1829 for an informal communion service.(10) They gathered as like minded, for fellowship, having at first no aim or intention of starting a new denomination or sect. The simple intention was of meeting with one another in a fellowship founded on a Scriptural basis. As yet there was no idea of the separation of those possessing the truth, from contamination of other Christian groups who were too tolerant.

That evening at Fitzwilliam Square was the acknowledged beginning of the movement. The similarity to the origins of the House Church Movement is remarkable - a group of like minded men, with a conception of the church based on New Testament principles who saw not a priest officiating in the church, but the priesthood of all believers - the ministry shared between groups of men. This was a conscious rejection of denominational structures, an attempt to go back to the New Testament pattern - to begin again both in organisation and practice.

Another attempt to do this had been made one hundred years previously - in 1730 in Scotland.(11) A group known as the Glasites emerged as a breakaway group from the Presbyterian Church. Their meetings appear to have had some similarity with early Brethren groups, except that the Kiss of Peace and Foot Washing were regular practices, and Brethren meetings have always had a most decorous and unemotional tone. The reason could be that the Glasites were predominantly of working class status, whereas one very important aspect of the Brethren has been the predominantly upper middle class and professional background of their adherents. Some were members of the aristocracy. Again a marked similarity is seen between the Brethren and members of the House Church Movement, particularly in the Harvestime Churches.

In an article written by Dr J.H. Brookes (12) Dr Anthony Groves is recorded as stating that the original intention of the brethren who met together was to permeate the denominational churches with God's truth and a new interest in the Scriptures. This would be done by emphasising the neglected points of evangelical Christian doctrines such as -

> the infallibility of Scripture,
> the deity of Christ - His vicarious atonement,
> Redemption by the blood of Christ alone
> and received by faith alone.
> The certainty of Salvation
> and the second coming of Christ.

However, separation from the existing denominations soon followed - as such a concept of the church could not find acceptance within the established ecclesiastical traditions.

Ironside points out that the widespread view that the Brethren movement was founded on prophecy concerning the second coming of Christ was inaccurate. Rather the doctrinal emphasis was on the subject of the Holy Communion. (13) The early leaders felt there was nothing in the Scriptures which necessitated an ordained clergyman to preside at Communion Services. Accordingly their first meetings were to break bread simply together. It was also felt that the Lord's Supper was not the sole property of any one church, but

"...where two or three are gathered together in my name,
there am I in the midst of them." (Matthew 18:20)

The Brethren followed the custom of using initials only to refer to their leaders. Ironside states the idea behind this could have been the conspicuous shield of the individual so that God is the focal point of the work. (14)   A similar reticence is seen in the House Church Movement; there are no prominent individuals who stand out, but a group of men who, acting as Apostles, share the ministry with the same attitude of giving credit to God.

Both the Brethren Movement and the House Churches are fundamentalist in their approach - the Bible is the complete authority and foundation of all teaching and practice and is applicable in all contemporary situations as its teachings are made effectual by the activity of the Holy Spirit. In the Brethren the ideology of the Holy Spirit plays a considerable role. The meetings are conducted on charismatic lines, i.e. a man speaks when moved by the Spirit. The meetings had no pre-arranged form in the early days. The similarity, in concept, to the House Churches is clear - the difference in the two types of meetings stems from the interpretation of the word charismatic. To the Brethren this was the silent prompting of the Holy Spirit. To the House Churches it is the outward and vocal manifestation of the gifts of the Spirit together with such expressions of worship as hands lifted in the air, or hand clapping during the singing.

Leading from this distinction a contrast has been seen in the general outlook of the two groups. The modern House Church is essentially cheerful and outward looking; there is a prevailing mood of optimism in all the meetings - whereas the Brethren Assemblies with their exaggerated sense of decorum could be seen to be prohibitive and negative. An early pioneer, A.N. Groves, of the Plymouth Assembly, wrote to J.N. Darby in 1835 a letter strangely prophetic, in which he warned that the Brethren could become known "more for what they witnessed against than for what they witnessed for". (15) This has certainly materialised, as has meticulous attention to detail regardless of the spirit of the law. For example during the early years of the seventies, when women's fashion favoured the mini skirt, one member of a Brethren Assembly remarked it did not seem to matter how short was a girl's skirt so long as she had her head covered in the meeting.

In the first twenty years the Brethren Movement went through various stages of evolvement. Beginning as a fellowship of Christians, it then began to attract and draw Christians in from the denominational churches - this was seen as a protest against ecclesiastical traditions, but all were desiring to know a more vital experience of Christianity. Then as the movement became more defined and articulate an increased awareness came of its principles and boundaries - these rapidly became laws and points of disagreement. It is important to remember that the well known terms Exclusive and Open do not refer to willingness or otherwise to associate with other Christians but originally indicated either an Assembly which preserved the truth exclusively or one which was open to other ideas - seen by the exclusives to be heretical contamination. One of the saddest yet most important facets of the Brethren Movement is the number of quarrels and schisms which has rent the movement from its earliest days.

In the early days of the Charismatic Movement this new emphasis on the activity of the third person of the Trinity was seen as a means of reviving the whole Church. The leaders of the House Church Movement were never themselves associated with any group promoting Charismatic Renewal (such as the Fountain Trust) but arrived at their position on the nature of the Church independently. Nevertheless the ranks have been swelled by disillusioned members of churches who have become impatient waiting for the denominational structures to experience revival. Whether the tightening of discipline and doctrines, and the hardening of boundaries will ensue remains to be seen. It seems a distinct possibility when viewing the North Churches, but in the Harvestime groups there is no lack of spontaneity and expressions of co-operation with other Christian groups.

The basic point of conflict within the Brethren was the degree of toleration which could be exercised - practically this meant in the realm of church government. The question was whether the local church should be autonomous or whether there should be some form of central authority. Linked with that question was the point whether admittance to the Communion Service was the sole responsibility of local leaders or whether the opinions of other leaders should be followed. Throughout the years there was a distinct shift in Darby's thought - and he was one of the most influential voices - from the truth of the unity of all believers to the necessity to stand against error in the churches - and to become separated from such error.(16)

When dissociation from centuries of tradition occurs there is always the possibility to over-emphasise a particular point or introduce some new teaching One of the most important quarrels in Brethrenism centred around the teaching of Newton at Plymouth. As Embley points out(17) most Brethren agreed Newton's thought was heretical - but most did not agree with the subsequent steps that were taken to deal with the situation.

Today's leaders in the House Churches are probably aware of past mistakes and of the bad image quarrels amongst Christians present to society. In the North Churches where schisms have occurred it seems that the tendency has been for those separating to drift back into denominational churches rather than form a counter group. It is very difficult to obtain information on the subject of quarrels, particularly when personalities are involved, but at Worcester two schisms occurred in the space of four years. On the first occasion those who left continued to meet independently but eventually went into different denominational churches. On the second occasion those involved made no attempt to meet but found alternative places of worship. In the Harvestime Churches it has not been possible to discover any similar schism. Obviously discord has arisen from time to time, but the result seems to have been that of individuals leaving the fellowship or a leader moving to another sphere of work elsewhere, but no splinter groups continuing at variance. The most obvious tension exists in the Harvestime Churches between the London groups and the rest (see page 98) which are associated with Bryn Jones.

One aspect of the notion of separation from the world which is very similar in both Brethren thought and that of the House Churches is the separation from public affairs. Brethren have never entered into prominent positions in public life that one might expect considering the high level of their social standing and education. Similarly, in the House Church situation, it would be unusual to find a member in public office. The House Church means a full-time commitment for each member; however, this perhaps is not an impossibility for the future as there is undoubtedly a social awareness that has never been apparent in Brethrenism (with the exception of the contribution of such individuals as George Muller).

The Pentecostals

The most unusual aspect of the Pentecostal Movement is that it began, not as the result of the work or inspiration of one man or a group of men, but in sporadic outbursts all over the world. The leaders were made by the movement and thus the whole phenomenon is regarded as an act of God by the adherents. In the United States, from Kansas and Los Angeles, to Sweden, Great Britain and India little groups of people reported unusual religious activities.

Often referred to as the "tongues movement" - which term no doubt pinpointed the emphasis of the movement - other titles were used such as the Los Angeles Movement or the Barrett Movement. But a title acceptable to devotees and critics alike is the Pentecostal Movement.(18)

The Pentecostal Movement has its roots in the Holiness Movements of the 19th century, which were themselves an expression of a desire for a personal experience which went beyond that offered by formal religious practice. The scene was set by the work of Moody and Sankey and the American Revivalist meetings, the Keswick Convention in England and the explicit writings of R.A. Torrey on "the Baptism in the Spirit". Small groups claiming to have experienced spiritual baptism and speaking in tongues are known to have existed in the closing years of the 19th century. However, the Pentecostals themselves see 1901 as the year of the movement's birth - and the establishment of Bethel College, Topeka, Kansas as the foundation stone. Later the emphasis was to move to the disused stable at Azusa Street, Los Angeles, and Houston, Texas.

In England the impact of the Welsh Revival of 1904 played an inestimable part in the Pentecostal Movement which followed as believers hearing about the events in Wales expected the Welsh experience to extend to all parts of this country and beyond.

The Pentecostal League founded by Reader Harris spoke of a purifying cleansing baptism, but it was Reader Harris who was later to be one of the most voluble opponents of Pentecostalism, on the grounds of his objections to the emphasis on glossolalia.

Today it is interesting to note that some of the strangest opposition to the formation of House Churches comes from the adherents of the Charismatic Movement. Although for a different reason, instead of objecting to a specific religious practice the objection is to the breaking away from the denominational structure. In the case of the Harvestime groups the establishment of relationships based on submission has drawn much criticism.

The Early Pentecostals saw the movement as one of Revival for the whole Christian Church premature to the Rapture and the onset of the Last Days. In this country particularly, as Donald Gee points out, most of the leaders were Anglicans and remained so.(19) He also sees the floundering of the movement and the difficulties it encountered as being due to a lack of direction on the part of such leaders, a floundering which eventually moved towards the establishment of different Pentecostal sects.(20) It was eventually understood that it was impractical to attempt to contain new wine in old bottles. The House Churches have not waited for this to happen - their leaders began with an appraisal of what the church should be and acted accordingly, Both the North and Harvestime groups see the denominations only as obstacles blocking the ongoing work of God. The House Churches have learnt the lesson of what happened to the early Pentecostals who did not realise what results the Pentecostal experience would bring. Both Alexander Boddy and Cecil Polhill were in favourable circumstances. Bishop Moule was favourable to Boddy's convictions and both were able to travel extensively and attend Conferences. There was an overwhelming optimism that the Pentecostal Movement would be used to revive the churches. A glance at Church history would have shown that from the time of the Montanists such religious enthusiasm is more likely to be designated a heresy than accepted as a legitimate means to revive the Church. In this country the Pentecostal Movement encountered the most prejudiced and efficient opposition, more than in any other country(21); it survived but as separate sects which rapidly evolved into denominations.

In reading extracts of early Pentecostal meetings it is very obvious that the emphasis is on tongues and other ecstatic spiritual activity. Wesley had spoken of a second experience subsequent to that of conversion which was one of sanctification - so also did the Holiness preachers. Scenes were recorded in the Camp Revival meetings in the States during the latter half of the 19th century which rivalled any which later took place in the Pentecostal meetings.(22) Perhaps the Harvestime groups have unconsciously followed the pattern of camp meetings as a means of communicating their message and consolidating their members, without however the expressed emotion of a Revivalist meeting.

The difference claimed by the Pentecostal experience from the Baptism in the Spirit of the Holiness meeting was that this was a baptism with "signs following", i.e. tongues. It is very significant that each time it is recorded an individual received this experience it is always added each spoke in tongues. It was around the phenomenon of tongues speaking that all the controversy ebbed and flowed.

The early Pentecostal meetings were entirely spontaneous, and without any set order or direction. Frodsham records:

> "No one knew what might be coming, what God would do. All
> was spontaneous, all of the Spirit."(23)

The resulting chaos attracted the attention of the press and the condemnation of Christendom at large.

> "When one came through to conversion or Spirit baptism, the
> rejoicing broke loose with ringing hallelujahs! Praise the
> Lord! and the like. They embraced each other, shouted for joy
> and danced. The sermon and the explanation of the Word of God
> were pushed into the background in favour of the enthusiastic
> prayer and the subsequent feeling of happiness. The meetings
> were so full of noise and disorder to such a degree that the
> police interfered and arrested some of the leaders...."(24)

Another record states:

> "Arms move frantically, heads jerk so violently that some of
> the women are unable to keep their hats on."(25)

It seems to have been commonplace for people to writhe on the floor, to shout
and scream.

However, Bloch-Hoell points out that over the years the worship quietened
so that in 1947 a woman who attempted to interrupt a sermon by "singing in
the Spirit" was told by the preacher to be quiet.(26)

Despite the obvious excessive emotionalism of the meetings, one fact
stands out, that speaking in tongues was the essential outward sign of the
receipt of the Baptism in the Spirit. Today this is still echoed in the
teachings of the Pentecostal churches. However, in charismatic circles and
in the House Churches speaking in tongues is not considered an essential
element in receiving the experience of spiritual baptism. Probably the
tales of excessive emotionalism are still fresh and serve as a warning - and
probably for sociological reasons the Charismatic Movement of the fifties
and the House Church Movement have had an entirely different emphasis. There
has been a special interest in the word of prophecy - and the gift of tongues,
whilst not ignored, is almost avoided. There has been an added emphasis on
preaching and renewed interest in healing - but again without the spectacular
occurrences of the turn of the century.

Classical Pentecostalism has had a certain appeal for the working classes
and the underprivileged (such as the American Negro). The ability to speak in
tongues gave a certain status to the uneducated. The freedom to express
emotions no doubt accounts for the predominating numbers of women in the congregations. Meetings gave a welcome relief from life's tensions. Just as
in the primitive religions the events of daily life are enacted in worship
(e.g. fertility rites) so Pentecostal worship depicted life's traumas.(27)
Today's neo-Pentecostal has less of these needs and so the scenes of hysteria
have not been repeated.

Today there is a greater emphasis on relationships and on the psycho-
logical healing of the personality, and in the Harvestime Churches this has
been worked out in their distinctive teaching on authority and submission.

The early Pentecostal Movement was essentially a reaction against the
formalism of the Church, and against the middle class predominance in the
churches. Great satisfaction was derived when a Pentecostal leader emerged
who had no academic training but who simply claimed Divine appointment. This
seemed to prove to the congregation that education was not necessary in order

to be able to serve God - it gave them a feeling of equality with those in the denominational churches. One of the greatest Pentecostal leaders in this country was the Bradford plumber, Smith Wigglesworth, a man whose only book was the Bible. Others were Stephen and George Jeffreys of Moestey, South Wales, two of the leaders who were instrumental in 1908 in introducing the Pentecostal Movement to the regions of Wales which had seen the scenes of revival in 1904. Stephen Jeffreys was a miner and his brother George worked in the Cooperative Stores. Both became renowned evangelists. George, after attending the Pentecostal Missionary Union Bible School at Preston, eventually founded the Elim Church and was known to be one of the finest preachers of his day. Stephen without any training became a pioneer in evangelistic work of the calibre of Wesley and Whitfield(28), his work taking him not only through England but also to New Zealand, Australia, South Africa and the United States.(29) His son Edward said of his funeral at Maasteg,

> "It seemed as if the whole town had gathered to pay its last tribute because he was one of them, and never had he been ashamed to own it. From the bowels of the earth as a miner, God had honoured him to preach before great multitudes in the largest auditoriums throughout the world."(30)

In the House Church Movement a number of leaders are proud of their working class origins. Bryn and Keri Jones likewise come from a Welsh mining village, althoug it is notable that both were well educated and attended Bible College, and Keri trained to be a teacher.

Perhaps more contrasts and differences can be drawn with the early Pentecostals than comparisons. Certainly it seems that the neo-Pentecostals are determined to learn from the mistakes made at the beginning of the century. There is a stress on order following Paul's injunction, "Let all things be done decently and in order" (1 Corinthians, 14:40). An interesting illustration of how that command is maintained is found in the development of part of the worship, that of "singing in the Spirit" and that of the place of dancing in the service.

In the earliest accounts of Pentecostal groups this phenomenon of "singing in the Spirit" is found, each individual sings his own tune and words (usually tongues):

> "Many have received the gift of singing as well as speaking in the inspiration of the Spirit. The Lord is giving new voices, he translates old songs into new tongues, he gives the music that is being sung by the angels and has a heavenly choir all singing the same heavenly song in harmony. It is beautiful music, no instruments are needed in the meetings."(31)

Whereas in the early accounts it appears the atmosphere was one of emotion and even hysteria, today's demonstrations of this phenomenon are highly controlled. It occurs spontaneously, often at the end of a hymn or song, and stops spontaneously, and often the refrain of the song is sung again. In the Harvestime Churches the singing is often accompanied by chords on the guitars; it is always surprising when listening to the singing how it finishes - especially when the congregation numbers several thousand people, all stop as if to order. Often there is a definite melody which can be traced, and again, in a large auditorium the sound can be as waves coming first from one direction then another. This "singing in the Spirit" is held as Scriptural and many references are quoted which speak of singing to God e.g. Psalm 40:3, Isaiah 51:11 and Colossians 3:16.

Another development in worship which is at present gaining prominence, particularly in the Harvestime Churches, is dancing as part of worship. A counterpart to this practice can be traced in the United Society of Believers in Christ's Second Appearing, otherwise known as the Shakers. For them the dance was a later development of what was termed as "Shaking in the Spirit".(32) and in considering other aspects of the sect it appears the comparison ends with the dancing. The Shakers were a celibate, ascetic group totally withdrawn from the world.

The contemporary dancing has some variations. It can be spontaneous jumping up and down in time to the beat of the music, or dancing around the room holding hands, or dancing around in a circle. Dancing is frequently done with the children - all adds to the cheerful atmosphere of the service. More formal groups have also been formed who will enact in movement the story of a parable or the words of a hymn - this will be to a prearranged choreography. Such groups are not the prerogatives of the Harvestime Church but originally were introduced to this country from the States via the Fisherfolk group from the Episcopalian Church of the Holy Redeemer, Houston, Texas. Charismatic churches, such as St Michael's, C. of E., York and St John's, C. of E., Harborne, Birmingham, have initiated the formation of such groups. Various parallels are found in Scripture to authenticate the activity, such as David dancing before the Ark in the triumphal entry into Jerusalem (2 Samuel 6:14a).

It is obvious that these activities all depend upon a certain interpretation and application of the Biblical verses. Critics would see no point of contact at all between David dancing in a procession and the dancing which happens during the meetings. However, this is seen as a dimension of worship which is valuable as a further means of expression, and it is undoubtedly gaining in practice and popularity.

A final comparison in considering the three groupings of Methodism, Brethrenism and Early Pentecostalism with the House Church Movement is the position of women in all four types of church.

In early Methodism it was recognised that women had a testimony to give and they were allowed to do so, and were also permitted to give a short exhortation from the front of the church, or on the pulpit steps, never from the pulpit itself as that constituted preaching.(33)

John Wesley gave an early approval to such exhortations although it seems that in later years he found it difficult to make an exact decision concerning the appropriateness of women preachers. After Wesley's death many female preachers emerged, but in 1835 the Conference expressed its disapproval and thereafter women were discouraged from preaching. Although in the Primitive Methodist churches and in the Bible Christian groups, women continued to preach.

Wesley's correspondence with several of the prominent women of the early years shows his reserve but also his recognition of their gift for public speaking, and their effectual ministry to the "unsaved". In 1769 he wrote to Mrs Sarah Crosby:

> "...You may properly enough intermix short exhortations with prayer - but keep as far from what is called preaching as you can: therefore never take a text; never speak in a continued discourse without a break, about four or five minutes. Tell the people, 'We shall have another Prayer Meeting at such a time and place'."(34)

However, John Wesley recognised that whereas men had a call to the ministry, certain women undoubtedly had an extraordinary call. In 1777 he writes to Miss Mary Bosanquet:

> "I think the strength of the cause rests there - on your having an extraordinary call."(35)

In 1787 he sent Sarah Mallet a note authorising her to preach. Wesley's attitude to Sarah Mallet expressed in his letters shows that his reservations were crumbling somewhat. Overall he did take rather an indecisive position and circumstances did not match his ideology. Certain Methodist women like Mary Bosanquet (afterwards Fletcher), Elizabeth Evans and Mary Barritt, travelled about the country and held evangelistic services in the remote regions of Yorkshire and Derbyshire. To Sarah Mallet he wrote,

> "We give the right hand of fellowship to Sarah Mallet and have no objection to her being a preacher in our connection, so long as she preaches Methodist doctrine and attends to our discipline."(36)

It was certain that women such as Alice Cambridge, blind Margaret Davidson, Sarah Ryan, Ann Tripp, Ann Cutler, Elizabeth Collett and Mary Taft could not be ignored as thousands of lives were changed as a result of their preaching.

In the Brethren Assemblies the tradition for women to keep silent even to the extent of being unable to pray except in a ladies' prayer meeting probably stems from the days of the controversy at Plymouth between Newton and J.N. Darby. During the unpleasant period of disagreement the women ranged themselves on the sides of the two contestants. Darby at the time was an eligible bachelor of forty five, which no doubt added to the tense, highly charged atmosphere of the scene.(37)

Those who followed Darby created an unprecedented scene when by scraping their feet on the floor they silenced an unpopular speaker. Newton's female devotees copied out his tracts in the ensuing Tract War with Darby. Finally those supporting Darby refused to attend the funeral of Newton's wife. Such undignified exhibitionism led to the silencing of women in the Brethren communities. In recent years a woman has been permitted to sing but never to speak in a meeting.

By contrast women have enjoyed a very obvious role in Pentecostal circles. Pentecostal meetings have a definite appeal particularly for certain types of women. There has never been any thought of placing restrictions on female participation and activity. Amongst the early Pentecostalists the dramatic figure of Aimee Semple Macpherson stands out. Her methods of evangelism were too flamboyant to appeal to the reserved English nature, but in the United States she commanded a large following. When planes were still a novelty she used sign writing in the sky to advertise her meetings. Her services which were both evangelistic with an emphasis on healing were dramatic and sensational. She established her own denomination centred around the Angelus Temple in Los Angeles. She founded a Bible College and a private radio station in addition to a publishing business.(38) Following her death forty-two new churches were founded in two years.(39) Aimee Semple Macpherson was undoubtedly a showman; to be understood, as Donald Gee has remarked, she needs to be seen against the background of her time and her chosen place of residence - that is the melodramatic background of Hollywood.(40)

In more recent years the figure of the Revd Jean Darnell is conspicuous. Her itinerant ministry has become widely known especially in Britain, and she has been warmly accepted into most neo-Pentecostal circles. In local churches however preachers and leaders have tended to be male - no doubt as the early Pentecostals were mainly drawn from the working classes, women were not motivated towards positions of leadership, whereas the early Methodist women who became class leaders or preachers were of a fair standard of education.

In the House Church Movement there is an intentional absence of women figuring in the development of the House Churches. This is a conscious reaction to the past decades of overwhelming predominance of female activity in all church life, ranging from Catholic to Pentecostal. Subsequently no female figures have emerged, although in observing church and family life, women are neither repressed nor ignored (as could be said of the Brethren movement) and do make a contribution to the life of the church in a supporting role.

An interesting feature of the House Church Movement is that none of the elements of structure, ideals or patterns of worship are essentially new. Each has been anticipated by one or other of the early movements. What is new is that for the first time there is seen a mixture of the patriarchal element, the concept of a church based on a fellowship of personal relationships, without title or central organisation, and the emphasis of Holy Spirit activity in worship.

Every attempt at revival indicates a protest against the existing order and is an attempt to change or renew. The question is, will this occur in every generation? as a glance at the emergence of Methodism, the Brethren Movement and the early Pentecostals might indicate; or is the House Church Movement a product of the decade of the sixties? The 20th century has seen many changes which have challenged the Christian Church, the treat of ideologies such as Nazism and Communism, the rise of new nations in the Third World, the developments of technology and sociological change. Those who profess Christian convictions are concerned that the Church has a relevant part to play in contemporary society.

The overriding considerations of the churches in the 20th century have been those of unity. The Lausanne Conference on Faith and Order in 1947 made it clear that a united Church could only be brought about by a willingness to accept the unfamiliar. The W.C.C. assembly at New Delhi 1961 declared as definition of unity the idea that all Christians in every place should share a fellowship of prayer and a corporate life. The Ecumenical vision has been to rethink, reshape, and relinquish former traditions. In the denominations the desire for reunion of the churches has expressed both a wish to bury differences and the costliness of doing so which is seen in the length of time in this country alone it takes to achieve union.

As a protest against institutionalism the Charismatic Movement of the sixties sought to bring about a unity of Christians at grass roots level. As a strand of that neo-Pentecostal phenomenon the House Church Movement would also claim to be uniting Christians from different traditions.

All agree that the division of the Church into denominations is undesirable, but has the right approach been made to counteract the problem? Each denomination has its own concept of what the Church should be. Can it be that the House Churches, in particular the Harvestime Churches, with their developed concept of the Church, will be able to retain their spontaneity in succeeding generations? Is this latest example of recurrent revival likely to take a stereotyped form as time goes on? The machinery of organisation is there, albeit at present it operates on personal relationships, but if these were taken away an institutionalised structure could easily become established.

In conclusion it can be seen that Methodism, Brethrenism and early Pentecostalism all began from the motive of bringing a more vital relevant Christianity into the life of the Church. As the denominational churches refused to acknowledge their contribution each was forced through circumstances to separate. Only the House Churches have originated with the intention of developing as separate entities. They came into being as churches not as groups, seeking through their fellowships to enrich the denominations. Thus they earned censure and the accusation of creating schism.

A consideration of the House Church Movement must first give some attention to the society in which such a movement arose. A society in which, as was stated in the opening chapter, religion no longer plays a socially significant part, no longer does life have a religious orientation. Furthermore, the traditional religious institutions are suffering a steady decline. Man has indeed "come of age" and has no need of a supernatural God.

There are however variant interpretations of such a secularisation. Both Bryan Wilson and David Martin acknowledge the decline of institutional religion but, whereas Bryan Wilson maintains "Men act less and less in response to religious motivation"(1) but organise their lives according to empirical and rational principles which leave little room for personal religious affinities, David Martin sees mankind as saturated with "a luxuriant theological undergrowth which provides the working core of belief more often than is realised".(2) Religion therefore is by no means obliterated from society, but now belongs to the private and personal compartments of life.

Obviously arguments can be found to substantiate both points of view, probably depending on which sector of society is examined and to a certain extent on the questions asked. The House Churches have emerged as a defence against all aspects and interpretations of secularisation, against on the one hand a society run on intellectual criteria, and on the other a restatement of fundamentalist beliefs in the face of an upsurge of various metaphysical superstitions.

The denominational churches themselves have in their way helped the flow of secularisation, often in moves intended to retain their members and provide alternative options to the lure of worldly pleasures. So it can be seen that all the Methodist meetings were originally entirely of a religious nature, the prayer meeting, class meeting and the worship service. By the 1870s the pattern had changed and elements of social activities are noticed such as the Sunday School anniversaries and educational and informative meetings. It is noticeable that in the second half of the 19th century the new nonconformist churches were built on the style of the concert hall and town hall with a stage for the choir with the minister's place in the centre. It is significant how many Methodist chapels later became libraries or cinemas as mass entertainment surpassed what had once been the role of the churches. Although the House Church caters for every aspect of life, including the leisure activities, there is a firm pre-eminence given to the religious activities, worship and fellowship are all important and care is taken to maintain that priority.

One aspect of the secularisation of society has its roots in the story of the progress of the working classes. Centuries of servitude by the ordinary people were overthrown in a comparatively short period; society is now no longer dominated by a work-orientated ethic but by the pursuit of leisure and pleasure. For as long as possible the privileged classes sought to maintain their own comfortable existence at the expense of those labouring for them and salved their consciences by allowing them to attend Sunday evening worship. The coming of first the railways and then the internal combustion engine opened up new horizons for the poor. So that other choices than church were available to them and often were a more attractive way of spending leisure time.

The coming of the secular society brought a great freedom to many. There was a freedom of choice, often to live and to work where and how one pleased. The confines of the former society were broken, and intimate relationships are a matter of personal selection out of a range of casual acquaintances met in day to day experiences. Formerly in the presecular age man spent his life in one place of limited circumference and all his fellow inhabitants he knew well. Today's man needs the anonymity of the urban dweller for he could not get involved with every individual he met; he has the freedom to choose rather than suffer relationships thrust upon him.

However, the welcome privacy of anonymity can become a loss of identity, and man becomes a number on a computer card. The loneliness of the technological age leads to a searching for community. Society is more mobile now than at any other time in history. Relatives usually live some distance away, a progressive career often means several moves to different towns in a relatively short time. Man can become disillusioned with the wider strictures of society and begin to desire a structure of relationships in which there is security.

Many people join a House Church for such a feeling of security; they want to belong, to experience meaningful relationships with those who can be trusted.

Each type of House Church answers that need by providing a protective society to a degree that all social contact is provided by the House Church. In some cases community homes are established where those needing a sheltered environment give up their outside employment to work in the home. Others work for members of the fellowship who own businesses. In the Community House at Worcester, one of the North fellowships, is a full time chef, an ex-University student, an ex-nurse, a secretary, and an ex-shop assistant, each came disillusioned with their environment and seeking a measure of protection. It can of course be argued that such a protection is an artificial society and as such can only be used as a temporary respite if the personality is to regain its wholeness.

Within the pattern of life in the House Church is seen a withdrawal from things of the world. The world is inherently sinful and belongs to the devil, whereas those in the House Church are the redeemed and belong to God. In the Harvestime Churches it is emphasised the members are in the Kingdom of God, and quite separate from the world, and indeed from other churches. An analogy used by Bryn Jones at the Annual Conference in 1975 was the people who followed this teaching were like the three hundred who went on with Gideon (Judges 7:7).

A significant thesis has been suggested by George A. Lindbeck of Yale University. (3) He sees the future of the Christian Church most probably to lie in sectarianism. He suggests society will continue the process of secularisation, that in fact the world will gradually and probably over a long period become de-Christianised. Given these conditions, as social support disappears, it will become necessary for Christians to gather in mutually supportive groups.

In the search for community in the past two decades different expressions of commune have emerged - the flower people, the hippies, the drug subculture, each seeking for an assurance of security. The House Church fits into this pattern, which if Lindbeck's assumptions are correct, will continue to supply the framework of an all inclusive and exclusive society. To many this is seen as a retrograde step - the re-establishment of a clear code of ethics based on Biblical authority, the reinforcement of family order within a tight network of relationships in the church. An undoubted attempt to throw off the forces of secularisation and return to a society based on a theocracy, i.e. where God is in control! Bryan Wilson pointed out, "Revivalism promises a return to the decencies of the past, through a reassertion of fundamental truths".(4) He reaches a conclusion which is in line with that of Lindbeck:

> "It may be, that in response to the growing institutionalism,
> impersonality, and bureaucracy of modern society, religion will
> find new functions to perform - but that, perhaps would be not
> the religion which accepts the values of the new institutionalism,
> the religion of ecumenism, but the religion of the sects."(4)

In practical ways the House Churches are establishing tightly knit communities. It is common practice for church members to take the opportunity to buy houses in the same road. Such an arrangement could prove to be very expedient in the future. The church at South Chard was one of the forerunners in this respect as members gradually bought up houses as they became vacant, or built them on available pieces of land in the village.

Yet it can be seen that secularisation is far from completed yet. Although firm conclusions cannot be drawn from opinion polls, nevertheless certain indications can be seen: in National Opinion Poll 1970, 75 per cent claimed an allegiance to the Church of England and only 3 per cent stated they were non-religious. Butler and Stokes in their research in 1969 found 64 per cent claimed to be Anglicans.(5) However, whatever statistics regarding church attendance say, it seems inevitable that one's funeral is marked by a religious service. A civil cremation can be arranged but is still unusual and the Church holds the monopoly on burials.

The difference between the casual attendance at religious services and religious fervour is obvious. What is understood by religion - is it an observance of religious duty, or an understanding of the beliefs involved? Historically the understanding of the faith has been left to the few; the masses have always held at best vague ideas of doctrine. It has been the evangelical sector of the Church in more recent years which has endeavoured to produce an informed congregation, by longer sermons and the weekly Bible study. Certainly the members of sectarian groups are better informed than the average churchgoer. The Jehovah's Witnesses and the members of the Church of Jesus Christ of the Latter Day Saints are taught systematically the tenets of the faith.

All types of House Church likewise instruct their members. There is great emphasis on preaching, sermons are never less than an hour in length and sometimes more than two. Tapes of sermons are circulated to those who miss the service. The House Church member will know what he believes and why.

It is inevitable that a movement which provides an alternative church structure will receive considerable criticism from other Christian groups, particularly if a good proportion of the members have left the ranks of those groups to join such a movement. The Harvestime Churches have attracted much attention because of their spectacular growth, which in the space of approximately five years grew from about eight or ten churches, numbering perhaps fifty or sixty people at the most, to hundreds of fellowships with a total membership of around 40,000. On the whole, criticism has come from other neo-Pentecostals, who see the movement as a threat, both to the unity of the Charismatic Movement, and as a threat of a new breakaway schism.

Michael Harper voiced such criticism in the magazine Crusade in March 1976. Chiefly concerned with the issue of authority, Michael Harper stated the movement owed its teaching and ideas to the preaching of a South American evangelist, Juan Ortez from Argentina. He stated Ortez had a long and close association with the American group of churches known as the Christian Growth Mission. This group was formed to care for the thousands of "nomadic" Christians the charismatic renewal has produced in the States. Christians who have no disciplined church connections, who emphasise solely a spiritual experience which produces a situation typifying the situation described in 1 Corinthians. Accordingly the Christian Growth Movement attempted to give a new emphasis on a disciplined way of life, in the acknowledgement of spiritual shepherds.

In his article Michael Harper accused the leaders in this country of distorting Scripture by basing a principle of church structure on an allegory of David and Saul (Divine government versus democratic power) that Dr Ern Baxter introduced at the Conference in 1975. He further attacked the movement for following the teaching of Ortez and producing "mashed potato Christians", to use an illustration of Ortez, that is Christians who are so united and integrated that they have lost their individuality.

Any reliance of the movement upon Ortez is strongly refuted by the leaders of Harvestime, and when Ortez visited Bradford in 1978 none of those involved in the administration of the Harvestime Churches attended his meetings. They are moreover eager to point out an important difference occurs in the realm of discipline. Juan Ortez and his followers practise a one to one chain of discipleship, that is every member of the church has his place, the one above him has spiritual authority and is the one to whom he turns for counsel; for the one below him he in turn bears spiritual responsibility. In the Harvestime movement there is no one to one discipleship - the Elders of the church carry the responsibility of a group of people, followed by the house group leaders. Where there is a need for discipline the matter will be discussed first with the house group leader, then one of the Elders. This clear statement of policy could be an attempt to rid the movement of the nickname "The Pyramid" with which it has been dubbed in recent years. Certainly it is now very difficult to trace any hierarchy - and any questions asked as to who relates, or is submitted to whom, seem to end in confusion.

An exception to the above rule are the fellowships which are developing from the work of the church at Merryfield House, Witney. That particular church follows the principles of Ortez and has a one to one discipleship in operation. This exception can be explained when it is seen that the chain of Apostles from that church leads to personalities in the United States.

However, the leaders of the Harvestime Churches claim that two years after the publication of the article in <u>Crusade</u>, Michael Harper met with them at a Conference. Differences were discussed and Michael Harper offered to publish a retraction of what he had written - that offer was refused.(6)

That there is a polarisation of ideas between the Harvestime groups and other neo-Pentecostals cannot be denied. Authority is only one issue, basically the concept of the church is at stake, and the issue is that which lies between church and sect.

Michael Harper and like minded people such as the Fountain Trust organisation represented are dedicated to renewal within the existing denominations. The question is, can the churches be renewed? or whether to use a frequently heard expression, "new wine must have new wineskins". Those in all types of House Church would maintain the churches cannot be renewed, but individuals out of every church are coming together in the fellowship of the very wide influence of the Charismatic Movement. The truth of this statement is born out by observation. In most towns in this country, although it may not be possible to find any churches which are open to the Charismatic Movement, it is easy to find a house meeting made up of members of many denominational churches, coming together during the week to worship, whilst still retaining their allegiance to the denominational churches. One could pose the question, what will happen next? how can the Charismatic Movement develop in future? and from that move on to consider:

Why have the House Churches developed in their present form? Their growth rate indicates their significance on the contemporary ecclesiastical scene. The answer can be seen to lie in two areas - the one theological, the other sociological.

Why are people so disillusioned as to leave the denominational churches? Many believe the traditional forms of worship and traditional structures of leadership should be renewed. The liturgical movement has gone so far, but some are impatient for more far reaching alterations. It seems many consider that the Christian faith should consist of more than a weekly attendance at a place of worship. In many denominational churches members have only a superficial knowledge of each other. The average church situation has been compared to a set of billiard balls, which as they click together resemble the church congregation bidding the time of day as they meet on Sunday only to separate to go their own ways until the following week.(7) It is felt that the Christian community should be like Paul's analogy of the body, each member having an important part to play (1 Cor. 12:12-26).

This constant use of the analogy of the body is interesting, as the most frequent accusation levelled at the House Churches by the denominations is that of fragmenting the body. However, they would maintain they are accomplishing the reverse by drawing God's people together. When the idealism of this picture of unity is challenged, the adherents of the Harvestime Churches would say as the whole church structure is based on relationships it is difficult for them to consider a major dispute of disagreement, since they are totally committed to each other and related as they say like brothers. As they share the same beliefs, visions and ideals, and as their whole relationships are based upon submission, any division or schism is hardly possible. If the submission is real, once a decision has been made on any issue, all must follow and agree. The alternative would be fragmentation. It has been expressed to me that it is difficult to explain the degree of commitment and loyalty that the leaders have for each other.(8)

Without articulated traditions so much depends upon the personalities involved. One can only wait to watch future events. Most of the leaders at present are in the early forties age range, but what will happen as the leadership passes to others? Will they feel the same degree of loyalty to each other?

Again there is the question of orthodoxy. The Harvestime Churches stand in the mainstream of fundamentalist, Pentecostal tradition, and probably will remain so for the present generation of leadership. The next generation is an unknown quantity. The two other types of House Church have already demonstrated deviant practice or belief - Chard with their Jesus only baptismal formula and Mr North's interpretation of New Birth.

Bryan Wilson makes an interesting remark in writing on the Christadelphian Movement.(9) He states that where individual churches are autonomous there is more likelihood of schisms arising. During 1977 a near schism was avoided between Bryn Jones and his associates and a group of fellowships centred around London and the Home Counties. This group of fellowships under the apostleship of John Noble, Maurice Smith, Gerald Costes, Graham Perrins and formerly David Mansell had always placed a greater emphasis on the personal freedom of a Christian than on the structure and authority of the Church. The issues in question centre around the interpretation of Law and Grace - the London groups having a more liberal approach than those who are associated with Bryn Jones.

The tension came to a head over two issues. One was a personal difference between David Mansell and John Noble. From that time David Mansell moved up to Bradford to work with Bryn Jones and his associates.

The second issue concerned John Noble's public comments to a group of Elders who had gathered to discuss the outworking of the personal life of a Christian, where he condoned the practice of masturbation. A reaction of horror was immediately seen; Arthur Wallis wrote to Noble saying such teaching was of "another spirit" and fellowship could not continue until this matter was resolved satisfactorily. Great offence was taken to the reference to "another spirit" by Noble and his associates, and they indicated they wished the letter to be withdrawn. For a time the two groups moved independently, but during 1979 moves were made to close the gap.

The sharp reaction by the leaders at Bradford to such a radical pronouncement was not surprising. Far reaching changes in attitudes have resulted from events such as the Wolfenden Committee on Homosexual Offences and Prostitution 1956, the Obscene Publications Act 1959 and the Abortion Act of 1967. The evangelical sector of the Church has rallied under such banners as the Festival of Light and is headed by the personalities of Lord Longford and Mary Whitehouse. Their concern is to maintain the institution of the Christian family with the accompaniments of traditional morality. The Harvestime Churches would not wish in any way to be seen to deviate from the evangelical line. Such a statement could only cause misunderstanding and criticism and as upholders of orthodox evangelical tradition they could not allow that to happen.

Such incidents illustrate how easily fragmentation could occur, particularly where local churches have their idiosyncrasies. It has previously been noted in the chapter on case histories that the Church at Merryfield House has a different method of disciplining. The fellowships in London and the Home Counties have a stronger emphasis on freedom than on authority. Their Apostles do not maintain such a close contact with their local churches but are simply available if needed. Their meetings are less structured and more spontaneous. Regular organised patterns are avoided, and their fellowships are based on groups of friends and families who gather together, sometimes on Sundays, sometimes during the week. The basis is friendship rather than authority. These groups have their own magazine, Fulness. The existence of such diversity coupled with the lack of central organisation and articulated tradition could easily lead to disintegration. The fact that the Harvestime Churches are held together by personal relationships, which they see to be their strongest asset, could prove to be their breaking point. Their leaders would maintain God establishes their relationships and so they will never break. One can only counter that with the words of Gamaliel, Acts 5:38,39.

On the other hand, despite the protestations of denial, clear affiliations are seen between the house churches across the country. The leaders' Conferences, International Conferences and the Annual Conference have all been organised from Church House, Bradford. The machinery is there, it appears for an efficient denominational system; if the present spontaneity were to wane it would require very little change or effort for another stereotyped organisation to appear.

A mark of the Harvestime Churches is the emphasis on shepherding which could, and in some places has given rise to a patriarchal attitude. This is obviously more pronounced in some churches than others, but already there are churches where young couples have to seek the permission of the Elders before they become engaged. It is interesting to speculate how this will develop. At best shepherding is an expression of deep personal trust between members and Elders, but could this lead to an authoritarian repression? There have always been incipient dangers in any situation where divine inspiration is claimed. The expression heard constantly is "Listen to what God is saying!" This virtually seems to mean what the Elders are saying either in personal conversation or in the preaching. That the members are conditioned to obey is very obvious from for instance the prompt response when an appeal for money is made. The church at Solihull was asked to raise £10,000 to buy the bookshop which was then rented. Three weeks later an offering was taken of £5,500. This was from about one hundred people, most of whom were married couples. Such offerings are in addition to the tenth already tithed from income.

As the Elders claim to voice the revelation of God the possibilities are open for many ways of development. Each declaration of what God is now saying is followed enthusiastically and without question. It seems a sermon is accepted totally as God's message to the church, with comments as to how wonderful, how new or exciting the message is.

However, in practice it can happen that two individuals can be equally certain God is speaking to each in a different way. In that case if neither will submit it follows one will leave the house church fellowships. A situation occurred in the West Country where the outcome resulted in one couple leaving the church and another moving to Bradford to a new sphere of work. Such incidents are very difficult to research as members are bound by loyalty not to speak about the church or any of the dissensions that take place. All that can be noted is certain people once in prominence withdraw suddenly but again it is impossible to ascertain how often this happens.

To establish why House Churches have emerged, a consideration of some of their origins may indicate the answer. Some were instances of disillusioned members leaving an unsympathetic church, others were examples of ministers resigning, but all mirrored tension and stress, revolving often around the personalities concerned. There were doctrinal issues, but were these uppermost? In another situation with other individuals would a working solution have been resolved? Perhaps not always. The traditional attitude of the Brethren movement, for example, towards Pentecostalism caused many now in the forefront of the House Church Movement to leave their Brethren Assemblies. Mr and Mrs Sid Purse of South Chard were amongst the first. It is easy to judge an issue after the event, but how far has the House Church Movement been coloured by the perspectives of those responsible for its initiation? Certainly Bryn Jones was an enthusiastic young evangelist before he came into contact with the men from the Christian Growth Ministries in Florida. From the time Dr Ern Baxter spoke in 1975 a fresh impetus has been seen. It is hard to escape the conclusion that such a movement is very good for those at the top of the pyramid, as it were, the Apostles. Again it was very difficult to obtain a clear statement as to how the Apostles and even local Elders are appointed. To say the Elders' ministry becomes apparent, the Apostle is recognised as being set apart by God is rather vague. Presumably a man's talents could be hidden for years. The Platform speakers at the Conference (all of whom have Apostle status) have been known to share their former reserve with each other and their reluctance to work together, claiming that God, in teaching them to submit to each other, has taught them to work together in brotherly love. Further they have no satisfactory answer to the accusation of schism. To say God is bringing his people together is not an objective answer. The situation is that like minded people are moving together in ways they believe God is directing. Some of these have left their former churches. It would be more objective to admit this is in essence a new sect.

In all types of House Church the policy must be coloured by the leader's perspectives. This is the criterion within which each works, which gives the particular characteristics peculiar to each. This is seen most clearly in the way Mr G.W. North has imbued the fellowships he has influenced with his particular ideas of personal holiness.

All types of House Church emphasise the wickedness of the world and the necessity for withdrawal and total commitment to their particular form of fellowship. Possibly unconsciously if not intentionally this is done to ensure a willing co-operation on the part of members. After all, if the world were not so wicked it would not be necessary for total withdrawal and commitment to those particular tenets of belief and practice. There is certainly a tendency to see nothing of goodness in the world - the phrase "She's not a Christian but she's quite nice" perhaps sums up the assumption. However, it must be stated that attitude is not only found in the House Churches but in evangelical circles also.

Is it possible that God is in fact speaking in a new way to the Harvestime Churches and causing a new movement the kind of which has not been seen since the first Pentecost, or is the movement largely based on the subjective experience of a group of men who have the enthusiasm to inspire others?

The others seem to want to be inspired. A characteristic of all three types of House Churches is the obvious happiness of the members. In a way which is difficult to define the members of the churches resemble each other, that is it is easy to pick out in a crowd, groups which go to a house church. That can partly be explained because each family lives in a very similar way to the others in the church. In the Harvestime Churches a great deal of teaching emphasis has been on how one should behave and live. There have been many books the members have been instructed to read, books on how to be a good wife, how to be a good husband. It is not surprising the members have a similar air or look about them. In the North fellowships the same applies, although there has not been the overt teaching. However, the three-cornered headscarves the women wear to meetings are almost a uniform.

One very dangerous area seems to be the threat to individuality, which is seen in the Harvestime Churches. Every personal wish has to be submitted before the Elders for approval before it can be acted upon. The Elders bring it to God and thus divine approval is obtained.

This seems to have far reaching undertones. The Reformation issues were fought for an individual to be able to approach God without a mediator, to think for himself as he read the Scriptures and to know personally the assurance of salvation without the vehicle of the sacraments of the church. Are the Harvestime Churches now threatening those individual privileges? This seems very like the mashed potato discipleship of Ortez.

Coupled with the question of individuality is the concern which was felt by the House Church leaders both on this side of the Atlantic and in those churches related to the Christian Growth Ministry for the many charismatic gypsies who emerged in the wake of the Charismatic Movement. These were individuals who, claiming a spiritual experience as their authority, drifted here and there with no church affiliation, yet demanding to be heard as each pronounced his own pet doctrines. The problem was never so acute here as in the States - but it was to counteract this unfortunate state of affairs that the teaching on authority and submission was instigated. Perhaps the remedy is now in turn in need of a counteraction. Certainly the Christian Growth Ministries have not had the continuing emphasis that God is telling his people to move out of the denominational churches.

The emaphsis on male authority also has its roots in the matriarchal society of the States. In England too in most church situations women have been predominant in managing church affairs, in the States the shortage of men was more pronounced. Accordingly men like Demos Shakarian began the FGBMFI for businessmen. In all types of House Church there is only male leadership, but again in the Harvestime Churches the emphasis on male authority seems to be more pronounced.

How far can the House Church Movement be viewed solely as a religious movement, or are there wider social implications? House Churches have arisen within an industrialised society and, in contrast to the definition of a sect described by Troeltsch and later Niebuhr, they have emerged from the ranks of the literate urban middle class.

In several ways can they be seen as protest movements? A protest against ecclesiastical tradition, with a strong anti-clerical bias. There is the tendency to view the Church as an outworn relic which has been overcome by the advance of secularisation.

Constantly new movements appear within the Church. In every generation appears a concern to revitalise some aspect of the religious life. For the past two decades there has been a striving to make Christianity relevant to modern society, but the House Church Movement appears to express a widening of concern which reaches beyond religious functions to family life and one's place in the social community.

David Martin has commented that "sectarial enthusiasts may be lucky and be disappointed" in their expectation of the second coming of Christ at the turn of the century, but "the development of secular powers has brought both Utopia and doom closer to sober reality than ever before".(11) All types of House Church offer a secluded security, an assurance of eschatological hope. They also tend to attract the lonely and the insecure.

Moreover, in past decades as institutional religion has declined there has been an upsurge of supernatural phenomena. Influences from the East, a renewed interest in psychic practices are countered by the emphasis in the House Church Movement on the supernatural acts of God, manifested in healing and in the operation of the vocal Pentecostal gifts in worship.

Society requires protesters and deviants in order to define its standards of normality. Historically Christianity has been well schooled in the tradition of protesting against the majority. So in the future a sectarian Christianity such as is found in the House Churches might well flourish.

Lindbeck foresees, despite the greater attraction of Catholicism and ecumenism, the inability of the churches to cope with the advanced pressures of secularisation. The institutional structures of the denominations were built to serve the mass of society, not cater for an exclusive grouping, so that it seems probable ecumenism will be absorbed into society and the bureaucratic churches. The future of Christianity will lie with those deeply committed to a sectarian faith who will survive through de-Christianisation processes.

Those in the House Churches could unite with his final statement when he speaks of

> "transcendent hopes that God will strip and unite his church
> for action in whatever times of trouble may lie ahead".(12)

Finally it may be noted, the early Christian Church itself was a fragmentation of Judaism, and throughout Church history new movements have arisen, broken away, but each continually sought a revival, a refreshing, a new experience of God.

102

NOTES

Chapter I

1. Bryan Wilson, "Secularisation and the Clerical Profession", in Joseph Faulkner (ed.), Religious Influence in Contemporary Society, Merrill, Columbus, Ohio, 1972, p. 510.

2. Ivan Reid, Social Class Differences in Britain, Open Books, London 1977, p. 205.

3. David Martin, Dilemmas of Contemporary Religion, Blackwell, Oxford 1978, p. 48.

4. Winston L. King, "Eastern Religions: A New Interest and Influence", in Joseph Faulkner (ed.), op. cit., p. 556.

5. David Martin, op. cit., p. 23.

6. Stephen Neill, A History of Christian Missions, Penguin, Middlesex, 1964, p. 572.

7. Hans Küng, On Being a Christian, Collins, London 1976, p. 484.

8. Michael Harper, As at the Beginning, Hodder and Stoughton, London 1965.

9. The story of the FGBMFI is told by Demos Shakarian, The Happiest People on Earth, Hodder and Stoughton, London 1978.

10. For my information on the history of the Charismatic Movement, I am particularly indebted to the account given in Martin Robinson, The Charismatic Anglican, unpublished M.Litt. thesis, University of Birmingham, 1976.

11. Tom Smail, Renewal, Fountain Trust, Esher, Surrey, June/July 1979, p. 4.

Chapter II

1. Interview with Keri Jones, Bradford, 1st December 1978.

2. Interview with Mr G.W. North, Birmingham, 25th April 1979.

3. Letter received from Andrew Jordan of South Chard, dated 4th July 1979.

Chapter III

1. Interview with Goos Vedder, Chester, 8th December 1978.

2. Interview with Stephen Wood, Solihull, 11th February 1979.

3. Interview with Brian and Pat Clarke, Solihull, 4th May 1979.

4. Interview with Dave Richards, Witney, 11th April 1979.

5. Cogges Church, so called because this was the site of an old abbey, known as Cogges Priory, which later became a vicarage.

6. A well known independent Baptist church, notable chiefly for its charismatic lifestyle and ministry.

7. Barney Coombs, a well known figure in charismatic circles, left Basingstoke to live in Vancouver, Canada, in 1977. He returns to this country at intervals.

8. Interview with Dave and Penny Orange, 3rd February 1979.

9. Interview with Ron Bailey, 28th February 1979.

10. Interview with Miss Elizabeth Ware and Mr Nick West, London, 22nd March 1979.

11. This is not the same house church as the Richmond Fellowship mentioned in the account of the Solihull Christian Fellowship.

Chapter IV

1. Interview with Keri Jones, Bradford, 1st December 1978.

2. Interview with Goos Vedder, Chester, 8th December 1978.

3. Interview with Brian Pullinger, Solihull, 22nd October 1978.

4. Interview with Ron Bailey, Birmingham, 7th February 1979.

5. Prof. W. Hollenweger, The Pentecostals, S.C.M. Press, London 1972, p.14.

6. Interview with David Orange, 3rd February 1979.

7. Letter from Andrew Jordan, received 5th July 1979.

8. Bryan Wilson, Religious Sects, Weidenfeld & Nicholson, London 1970, p. 26-38.

9. Ibid, p. 28.

Chapter V

1. A.D. Gilbert, Religion and Society in Industrial England, Longman, London and New York, 1976, p. 4.

2. Adam Clarke (ed.), Memoirs of the Wesley Family, 2nd ed., pp. 155-56, quoted in Gilbert, ibid, p. 18.

3. "Rules for a Helper" enunciated at 1744 Conference, quoted in The Works of John Wesley, M.A. Mason, London, 1810, Vol. 6, p. 30, quoted in Gilbert, ibid, p. 21.

4. L.F. Church, The Early Methodist People, Epworth Press, London, 1949, p.42.

5. Ibid, p. 150.

6. Ibid, p. 151.

7. John Wesley, Journal, ed. by J. Telford, Epworth Press, London 1909, Vol.3, p. 223, quoted in Church, ibid, p. 4.

8. H.A. Ironside, A Historical Sketch of the Brethren Movement, Zondervan Publishing House, Grand Rapids, Michigan, U.S.A. Issued London, Marshall Morgan Scott, 1941.

9. Ibid, pp. 10ff.

10. Peter L. Embley, "The Early Development of the Plymouth Brethren", cited in Patterns of Sectarianism, ed. B. Wilson, Heinemann, London 1967, p.213.

11. Ibid, p. 214.

12. Ibid, pp. 214-15.

13. H.A. Ironside, op. cit., p. 16.

14. Ibid, p. 18.

15. Peter L. Embley, op. cit., p. 224.

16. Ibid, p. 224.

17. Ibid, p. 241.

18. Nils Bloch-Hoell, The Pentecostal Movement, Universitets Forlaget, Oslo, Allen & Unwin, London 1964, p. 1.

19. Donald Gee, Wind and Flame, Assemblies of God Publishing House, Croydon 1967, p. 74.

20. Ibid, p. 88.

21. Ibid, p. 88.

22. Ibid, p. 4.

23. Stanley Frodsham, With Signs Following, Springfield, Missouri, 1946, p.36, quoted in Nils Bloch-Hoell, op. cit., p. 161.

24. Nils Bloch-Hoell, op. cit., p. 43.

25. Frederich G. Henke, The Gift of Tongues, quoted in Nils Bloch-Hoell, op. cit., p. 55.

26. Nils Bloch-Hoell, op. cit., p. 162.

27. Bryan Wilson, Religious Sects, World University Library, London 1970, p.22.

28. Donald Gee, op. cit., p. 137.

29. Ibid, p. 153.

30. Ibid, p. 196.

31. The Apostolic Faith, Sept. 1906, quoted in Hils Bloch-Hoell, op. cit., p. 142.

32. Bryan Wilson, op. cit., p. 203.

33. L.F. Church, More About the Early Methodist People, Epworth Press, London 1949, p. 137.

34. John Wesley, Letters, Epworth Press, London 1931, Vol. IV, p. 164.

35. Ibid, Vol. V, p. 257.

36. Zechariah Taft, Sketches of Holy Women, Kershaw, London, 1825-28, Vol. 1, p. 84, quoted in L.F. Church, op. cit. 33, p. 170.

37. P.L. Embley, op. cit., p. 234.

38. Nils Bloch-Hoell, op. cit., p. 181.

39. Donald Gee, op. cit., p. 209.

40. Ibid, p. 120.

Chapter VI

1. Bryan Wilson, Religion in Secular Society, Penguin, Middlesex, 1969, p. 10.

2. David Martin, The Religious and the Secular, Routledge & Kegan Paul, London 1969, p. 107.

3. George A. Lindbeck, The Sectarian Future of the Church, Yale, unpublished paper, 1971.

4. Bryan Wilson, op. cit., p. 49 and 263.

5. Ivan Reid, Social Class Differences in Britain, Open Books, London 1977, p. 204.

6. Interview with Keri Jones, Bradford, 1st December 1978.

7. Arthur Wallis, Annual Conference, Lakes Bible Week, August 1975.

8. Interview with Goos Vedder, 8th December 1978.

9. Bryan Wilson, Sects and Society, Weidenfeld & Nicolson, London 1961, p. 341.

10. Information given in interview by Ron Bailey, Birmingham, 7th February 1979.

11. David Martin, The Dilemmas of Contemporary Religion, Blackwell, Oxford 1978, p. 103.

12. George A. Lindbeck, op. cit., p. 8.

BIBLIOGRAPHY

A. Personal communications

My main sources of information were leaders, members and former members of the House Church Movement.

1. Interview, Brian Pullinger, Solihull, 22nd October 1978.
2. Interview, Keri Jones, Bradford, 1st December 1978.
3. Interview, Goos Vedder, Chester, 8th December 1978.
4. Interview, Dave and Penny Orange, Leamington Spa, 3rd February 1979.
5. Interview, Stephen Wood, Solihull, 11th February 1979.
6. Interview, Ron Bailey, 28th February 1979.
7. Interview, Miss Elizabeth Ware and Mr Nick West, London, 22nd March 1979.
8. Interview, David Richards, Witney, 11th April 1979.
9. Interview, G.W. North, Birmingham, 25th April 1979.
10. Interview, Pat and Brian Clarke, Solihull, 4th May 1979.
11. Letter received from Mr Andrew Jordan of South Chard, dated 4th July 1979.
12. Interview, Miss Pam Rimmer, Chester, 13th August 1979.

B. Periodicals

Crusade Magazine, Thirty Press Ltd., with Evangelical Alliance, London.

Fulness Magazine, available only through Harvestime Churches.

Renewal Magazine, issued by the Fountain Trust, 3a High Street, Esher, Surrey until Feb/Mar 1981. Now published by Edward England, ed. by Michael Harper.

Restoration Magazine, obtainable only through Christian Bookshops run by the Harvestime Churches or from the church members and certain branches of the Christian Literature Crusade Bookshops e.g. Birmingham.

C. Published Works

Abercrombie, N., Baker, J., Brett, S., Foster, J., "Superstitition and Religion: The God of the Gaps", in A Sociological Yearbook of Religion in Britain 3, ed. David Martin and Michael Hill, SCM Press Ltd., 1970.

Andrews, S., Methodism and Society, Longman, London 1970.

Bloch-Hoell, N., The Pentecostal Movement, Allen and Unwin, London 1964.

Church, L.F., The Early Methodist People, Epworth, London 1948.

Church, L.F., More About the Early Methodist People, Epworth, London 1949.

Cox, H., The Secular City, Penguin, Harmondsworth, Middlesex, 1968.

Currie, R., Gilbert, A., Horsley, L., Churches and Churchgoers, Clarendon, Oxford, 1977.

Davies, R., Rupp, G. (eds), A History of the Methodist Church in Great Britain, Vol. I. Epworth Press, London 1965.

Edwards, D.L., Religion and Change, Hodder and Stoughton, London 1969.

Faulkner, J.E. (ed.), Religion's Influence in Contemporary Society, Charles E. Merrill, Columbus, Ohio, 1972.

Gee, D., Wind and Flame, Assemblies of God Publishing House, Croydon 1967.

Gilbert, A.D., Religion & Society in Industrial England, Longman, London 1976.

Goodridge, R.M., "The Secular Practice and the Spirit of Religion", in Social Compass, Vol. 20, 1973.

Halsey, A.H., Change in British Society, Oxford University Press, Oxford 1978.

Harper, M., As at the Beginning, Hodder and Stoughton, London 1965.

Hollenweger, W.J., The Pentecostals, SCM Press, London 1976.

Homan, R., "Sunday Observance and Social Class", in A Sociological Yearbook of Religion in Britain 3, ed. David Martin and Michael Hill, SCM Press, London 1970.

Ironside, H., A Historical Sketch of the Brethren Movement, Zondervan Publishing House, Grand Rapids, Michigan, USA. Issued London, Marshall Morgan Scott, 1941.

Küng, H., On Being a Christian, Collins, London 1976.

Lindbeck, G.A., The Sectarian Future of the Church, Yale unpubl. paper, 1971.

Martin, D., A Sociology of English Religion, Heinemann, London 1967.

———— The Religious and the Secular, Routledge and Kegan Paul, London 1967.

———— Tracts Against the Times, Lutterworth, Guildford and London 1973.

———— A General Theory of Secularisation, Blackwell, Oxford 1978.

———— The Dilemmas of Contemporary Religion, Blackwell, Oxford 1978.

Mehta, V., The New Theologian, Weidenfeld and Nicholson, London 1965.

Neill, S., A History of Christian Missions, Penguin, Harmondsworth, Middlesex.

Niebuhr, R.H., The Social Sources of Denominationalism, Holt, New York 1929.

North, G.W., One Baptism, private publication, 1978.

Perman, D., Change and the Churches, The Bodley Head, London 1977.

Pickering, W., "Religion - A Leisure-time Pursuit", in A Sociological Yearbook of Religion in Britain, ed. David Martin, SCM Press Ltd.

———— "The Secularised Sabbath: Formerly Sunday; Now The Weekend", in A Sociological Yearbook of Religion in Britain 5, ed. M. Hill, SCM Press 1972.

Rawlinson, A.E.J., Problems of Reunion, Eyre and Spottiswoode, London 1950.

Reid, I., Social Class Differences in Britain, Open Books, London 1977.

Robinson, M., The Charismatic Anglican, unpubl. M.Litt. thesis, University of Birmingham 1976.

Scharf, B.R., The Sociological Study of Religion, Hutchinson, London 1970.

Schwartz, G., Sect Ideologies and Social Status, University of Chicago Press, Chicago and London 1970.

Shakarian, D., The Happiest People on Earth, London 1978.

Skevington Wood, A., The Burning Heart, The Paternoster Press, Exeter 1976.

Weber, M., The Sociology of Religion, Methuen, London 1965.

Wesley, J., The Letters of the Revd. John Wesley, ed. John Telford, Vol. I-VIII, Epworth Press, London 1931. Reprinted 1960.

Wilson, B.R., Sects and Society,Heinemann, London 1961.

————— Patterns of Sectarianism, Heinemann, London 1967.

————— Religion in Secular Society,Penguin, Harmondsworth, Middlesex, 1969.

————— Religious Sects, Weidenfeld and Nicholson, London 1970.

————— Contemporary Transformations of Religion, Oxford University Press, 1976.

STUDIEN ZUR INTERKULTURELLEN GESCHICHTE DES CHRISTENTUMS
ETUDES D'HISTOIRE INTERCULTURELLE DU CHRISTIANISME
STUDIES IN THE INTERCULTURAL HISTORY OF CHRISTIANITY

Herausgegeben von/edité par/edited by

Richard Friedli
Université de Fribourg

Walter J. Hollenweger
University of Birmingham

Hans-Jochen Margull
Universität Hamburg

Band 1 Wolfram Weiße: Südafrika und das Antirassismusprogramm. Kirchen im Spannungsfeld einer Rassengesellschaft.

Band 2 Ingo Lembke: Christentum unter den Bedingungen Lateinamerikas. Die katholische Kirche vor den Problemen der Abhängigkeit und Unterentwicklung.

Band 3 Gerd Uwe Kliewer: Das neue Volk der Pfingstler. Religion, Unterentwicklung und sozialer Wandel in Lateinamerika.

Band 4 Joachim Wietzke: Theologie im modernen Indien - Paul David Devanandan.

Band 5 Werner Ustorf: Afrikanische Initiative. Das aktive Leiden des Propheten Simon Kimbangu.

Band 6 Erhard Kamphausen: Anfänge der kirchlichen Unabhängigkeitsbewegung in Südafrika. Geschichte und Theologie der äthiopischen Bewegung. 1880-1910.

Band 7 Lothar Engel: Kolonialismus und Nationalismus im deutschen Protestantismus in Namibia 1907-1945. Beiträge zur Geschichte der deutschen evangelischen Mission und Kirche im ehemaligen Kolonial- und Mandatsgebiet Südwestafrika.

Band 8 Pamela M. Binyon: The Concepts of „Spirit" and „Demon". A Study in the use of different languages describing the same phenomena.

Band 9 Neville Richardson: The World Council of Churches and Race Relations: 1960 to 1969.

Band 10 Jörg Müller: Uppsala II. Erneuerung in der Mission. Eine redaktionsgeschichtliche Studie und Dokumentation zu Sektion II der 4. Vollversammlung des Ökumenischen Rates der Kirchen, Uppsala 1968.

Band 11 Hans Schoepfer: Theologie der Gesellschaft. Interdisziplinäre Grundlagenbibliographie zur Einführung in die befreiungs- und polittheologische Problematik: 1960-1975.

Band 12 Werner Hoerschelmann: Christliche Gurus. Darstellung von Selbstverständnis und Funktion indigenen Christseins durch unabhängige charismatisch geführte Gruppen in Südindien.

Band 13 Claude Schaller: L'Eglise en quête de dialogue.

Band 14 Theo Tschuy: Hundert Jahre kubanischer Protestantismus (1868-1961). Versuch einer kirchengeschichtlichen Darstellung.

Band 15 Werner Korte: Wir sind die Kirchen der unteren Klassen. Entstehung, Organisation und gesellschaftliche Funktionen unabhängiger Kirchen in Afrika.

Band 16 Arnold Bittlinger: Papst und Pfingstler. Der römisch katholisch - pfingstliche Dialog und seine ökumenische Relevanz.

Band 17 Ingemar Lindén: The Last Trump. An historico-genetical study of some important chapters in the making and development of the Seventh-day Adventist Church.

Band 18 Zwinglio Dias: Krisen und Aufgaben im brasilianischen Protestantismus. Eine Studie zu den sozialgeschichtlichen Bedingungen und volkspädagogischen Möglichkeiten der Evangelisation.

Band 19 Mary Hall: A quest for the liberated Christian, Examined on the basis of a mission, a man and a movement as agents of liberation.

Band 20 Arturo Blatezky: Sprache des Glaubens in Lateinamerika. Eine Studie zu Selbstverständnis und Methode der »Theologie der Befreiung«.

Band 21 Anthony Mookenthottam: Indian Theological Tendencies. Approaches and problems for further research as seen in the works of some leading Indian theologians.

Band 22 George Thomas: Christian Indians and Indian Nationalism 1885-1950. An Interpretation in Historical and Theological Perspectives.

Band 23 Essiben Madiba: Evangélisation et Colonisation en Afrique: L'Héritage scolaire du Cameroun (1885-1965).

Band 24 Katsumi Takizawa: Reflexionen über die universale Grundlage von Buddhismus und Christentum.

Band 25 S.W. Sykes (editor): England and Germany. Studies in theological diplomacy.

Band 26 James Haire: The Character and Theological Struggle of the Church in Halmahera, Indonesia, 1941-1979.

Band 27 David Ford: Barth and God's Story. Biblical Narrative and the Theological Method of Karl Barth in the Church Dogmatics.

Band 28 Kortright Davis: Mission For Caribbean Change. Caribbean Development As Theological Enterprise.

Band 29 Origen V. Jathanna: The Decisiveness of the Christ-Event and the Universality of Christianity in a world of Religious Plurality. With Special Reference to Hendrik Kraemer and Alfred George Hagg as well as to William Ernest Hocking and Pandip eddi Chenchiah.

Band 30 Joyce V. Thurman: New Wineskins. A Study of the House Church Movement.